© **Copyright 2020 by Rolando Weller - All rights reserved.**

The information provided herein is stated to be truthful and consistent, in that any liability, in terms of inattention or otherwise, by any usage or abuse of any policies, processes, or directions contained within is the solitary and utter responsibility of the recipient reader. Under no circumstances will any legal responsibility or blame be held against the publisher for any reparation, damages, or monetary loss due to the information herein, either directly or indirectly. Respective authors own all copyrights not held by the publisher.

In no way is it legal to reproduce, duplicate, or transmit any part of this document in either electronic means or in printed format. Recording of this publication is strictly prohibited and any storage of this document is not allowed unless with written permission from the publisher. All rights reserved.

The trademarks that are used are without any consent, and the publication of the trademark is without permission or backing by the trademark owner. All trademarks and brands within this book are for clarifying purposes only and are owned by the owners themselves, not affiliated with this document.

This Book is provided with the sole purpose of providing relevant information on a specific topic for which every reasonable effort has been made to ensure that it is both accurate and reasonable. Nevertheless, by purchasing this Book you consent to the fact that the author, as well as the publisher, are in no way experts on the topics contained herein, regardless of any claims as such that may be made within. It is recommended that you always consult a professional prior to undertaking any of the advice or techniques discussed within.This is a legally binding declaration that is considered both valid and fair by both the Committee of Publishers Association and the American Bar Association and should be considered as legally binding within the United States.

# CONTENTS

- INTRODUCTION ............................................................................................................. 6
- Advantages Of Using Instant Air Fryer ..................................................................... 6
  - 1. More Healthy Cooking ......................................................................................... 6
  - 2. Quicker Food ......................................................................................................... 6
  - 3. Versatility ............................................................................................................... 6
  - 4. Space Saver ............................................................................................................ 7
  - 5. Easy to use ............................................................................................................. 7
  - 6. Ease of Clean Up ................................................................................................... 7
  - 7. Energy Efficiency .................................................................................................. 7
- Breakfast recipes ........................................................................................................... 8
  - Air Fryer Donuts ....................................................................................................... 8
  - Cinnamon Banana Bread ......................................................................................... 9
  - Cheese Frittata ........................................................................................................ 10
  - Healthy Pop Tarts ................................................................................................... 11
  - Breakfast Bombs ..................................................................................................... 12
  - Fried vegetables ...................................................................................................... 13
  - Tasty Baked Eggs .................................................................................................... 14
  - Breakfast Egg Bowls ............................................................................................... 15
  - Delicious Breakfast Soufflé .................................................................................... 16
  - Air Fried Sandwich ................................................................................................. 16
  - Rustic Breakfast ...................................................................................................... 17
  - Bacon Wrapped Filet Mignon ............................................................................... 18
  - Omni air fryer oreos ............................................................................................... 19
- Air Fryer Lunch Recipes ............................................................................................ 20
  - Chicken, Corn, Beans and Quinoa Casserole ...................................................... 20
  - Chicken and Zucchini Lunch Mix ........................................................................ 21
  - Chicken and Corn Casserole ................................................................................. 22
  - Easy Chicken Lunch ............................................................................................... 22
  - Salmon and Asparagus .......................................................................................... 23
  - Turkey Burgers ....................................................................................................... 24
  - Coconut and Chicken Casserole ........................................................................... 25
  - Zucchini Casserole ................................................................................................. 26
  - Sweet Potato Lunch Casserole .............................................................................. 27
  - Air Fried Thai Salad ............................................................................................... 28
  - Special Lunch Seafood Stew ................................................................................. 29
  - Bacon Pudding ........................................................................................................ 30
  - Meatballs Sandwich ............................................................................................... 31
  - Beef Stew ................................................................................................................. 32
  - Cheese Ravioli and Marinara Sauce .................................................................... 33

- Turkey Cakes .................................................................................................................... 33
- Lunch Pork and Potatoes ................................................................................................ 34
- Creamy Chicken Stew ..................................................................................................... 34
- Italian Eggplant Sandwich ............................................................................................. 35
- Succulent Lunch Turkey Breast ..................................................................................... 36
- Steaks and Cabbage ........................................................................................................ 37
- Stuffed Meatballs ............................................................................................................ 38
- Meatballs and Tomato Sauce ......................................................................................... 39
- Sweet and Sour Sausage Mix ......................................................................................... 40
- Bacon and Garlic Pizzas ................................................................................................. 41
- Corn Casserole ................................................................................................................. 42
- Lunch Potato Salad ......................................................................................................... 43
- Lentils Fritters ................................................................................................................. 44
- Prosciutto Sandwich ....................................................................................................... 45
- Japanese Chicken Mix .................................................................................................... 46
- Easy Hot Dogs .................................................................................................................. 46
- Delicious Chicken Wings ............................................................................................... 47
- Beef Lunch Meatballs ..................................................................................................... 47
- Chinese Pork Lunch Mix ................................................................................................ 48
- Chicken Kabobs ............................................................................................................... 48
- Turkish Koftas ................................................................................................................. 49
- Tasty Cheeseburgers ....................................................................................................... 49
- Philadelphia Chicken Lunch ......................................................................................... 50
- Pasta Salad ....................................................................................................................... 51
- Delicious Beef Cubes ...................................................................................................... 52
- Hash Brown Toasts ......................................................................................................... 53
- Fish And Chips ................................................................................................................ 53
- Lunch Chicken Salad ...................................................................................................... 54
- Lunch Fajitas ................................................................................................................... 55
- Macaroni and Cheese ..................................................................................................... 56
- Chicken Pie ...................................................................................................................... 57
- Buttermilk Chicken ........................................................................................................ 58
- Hot Bacon Sandwiches ................................................................................................... 59
- Fresh Chicken Mix .......................................................................................................... 60
- Chicken Sandwiches ....................................................................................................... 60
- Scallops and Dill ............................................................................................................. 61
- Lunch Special Pancake .................................................................................................. 61
- Lunch Shrimp Croquettes .............................................................................................. 62

Poultry recipes ........................................................................................................................ 63
- Chicken and Rice ............................................................................................................. 63

- Chicken wings .......................................................................................................... 64
- Rotisserie chicken .................................................................................................. 65
- Tasty Chicken Tandoori ....................................................................................... 66
- Thyme turkey breast ............................................................................................. 67
- Caribbean chicken ................................................................................................. 68
- Turkey Meatballs ................................................................................................... 69
- Buttered turkey wings .......................................................................................... 69

## Beef and Lamb recipes ............................................................................................. 70
- Lamb chops ............................................................................................................. 70
- Roast beef ................................................................................................................ 70
- Seasoned beef roast ............................................................................................... 71
- Filet mignon ............................................................................................................ 72
- Artichoke pepper beef .......................................................................................... 72
- Air fryer beef meatballs ....................................................................................... 73
- Cheese stuffed pork chops ................................................................................... 74
- Olive feta beef ........................................................................................................ 75
- Lamb scallop casserole ........................................................................................ 75

## Pork Recipes ................................................................................................................. 76
- Seasoned pork loin ................................................................................................ 76
- Glazed pork ribs ..................................................................................................... 77
- Stuffed pork roll .................................................................................................... 78
- Herb butter pork chops ........................................................................................ 79
- Pork stew ................................................................................................................. 80
- Meatloaf ................................................................................................................... 81
- Cajun pork chops ................................................................................................... 82
- Jerk pork butt ......................................................................................................... 82
- Pork sausage and peanut sauce ......................................................................... 83

## Seafood and fish recipes ........................................................................................... 84
- Baked tilapia ........................................................................................................... 84
- Baked shrimp scampi ........................................................................................... 84
- Greek fish ................................................................................................................ 85
- Tasty crab cakes ..................................................................................................... 86
- Simple salmon patties .......................................................................................... 86
- Avocado shrimp ..................................................................................................... 87

## Vegetarian Recipes ..................................................................................................... 88
- Avocado fries .......................................................................................................... 88
- Spinach bake .......................................................................................................... 89
- Broccoli fritters ...................................................................................................... 89
- Air Fryer .................................................................................................................. 89
- Simple baked vegetables ..................................................................................... 90

- Parmesan brussels sprouts ..................................................................................... 91
- Stuffed tomatoes ................................................................................................... 92

## Snack and appetizer recipes ............................................................................. 93
- Haddock nuggets ................................................................................................... 93
- Herb Mushrooms ................................................................................................... 94
- Mashed Potatoes ................................................................................................... 95
- Cinnamon honey glazed sweet potato .................................................................. 96
- Creamy zucchini dip ............................................................................................. 97
- Healthy carrot fries .............................................................................................. 98
- Artichoke dip ........................................................................................................ 99
- Mix nuts ............................................................................................................. 100
- Ranch chickpeas ................................................................................................. 100

## Dessert recipes .................................................................................................. 101
- Carrot cake ......................................................................................................... 101
- Pumpkin muffin .................................................................................................. 102
- Banana Chocolate brownies .............................................................................. 103
- Blueberry cakes .................................................................................................. 104
- Sicilian cannoli ................................................................................................... 105
- Pear bread pudding ............................................................................................ 106
- Cherry crumble .................................................................................................. 107

# INTRODUCTION

At the touch of a button, the Instant Omni Plus Toaster Oven is perfect for home cooks who want fast, nutritious, easy meals every day ... The large capacity of 26 liters gives you plenty of room to do a lot of things: air fry, slow cook, dehydrate, roast, bake broil, reheat, proof, convection cook, rotisserie cook – and toast, of course – all the food you need to feed your family and friends.

With Golden Quartz technology and dual top and bottom heating elements, high-performance heating ensures crisp, golden results at any time. There's no need to calculate temperature, weight or time with a variety of one-touch cooking options. Just choose one of the 11 Smart Programs, and click start.

However, the Omni Plus Toaster Oven offers the flexibility to adjust settings to customize your culinary experience for your foodies out there. With Smart technology for your smart kitchen, you can switch from simple reheat to skilled cooking expertise with cooking temperatures ranging from room to 450 ° F.

The Omni Plus is so much more than just a toaster oven, it even comes with all the rotisserie cooking accessories that you need. Along with the rotisserie feature, the high performance convection oven produces juicy, tasty rotisserie dishes.

## Advantages Of Using Instant Air Fryer

### 1. More Healthy Cooking

So how can anything fry be healthy? FASHING! If you choose to use it, these devices can be used without any oil at all, or with just a tiny spritz.

Without the extra oil, you can fry frozen fries, onion rings, wings, and more and still get pretty crispy results. The frites from the air fryer were crispier but not dried out compared to using my microwave, so it was even more exciting to use to produce breaded zucchini wedges!

### 2. Quicker Food

Since they're smaller than an oven and fans blow the air around, they 're also cooking food quicker. It can take up to 20-30 minutes for an oven to preheat properly, whereas these fryers arrive at temperature within minutes.

I was really surprised that after 15 minutes, when they spend up to 45 minutes in the oven, my frozen fries are fine. You'll probably love this time saver if you need to prepare snacks or meals in a rush.

### 3. Versatility

This I think is my favorite air fryer feature. You can do that MUCH! Yeah, similar to an oven it cooks really well. But it can also bake (even cakes), broil, barbecue and stir fry! Feel like eating chicken and snow peas? Any of those is easy to render with. You can cook fresh and frozen food and even heat contaminants in it. I've made poultry, fish, casseroles, salads and a lot of assorted vegetables in mine. Some fryers come with external equipment, such as a rotisserie plate, grill pan or an elevated plate for frying. Dividable baskets mean that you can even prepare many items at once. It is amazing that so many things can be cooked in so many ways from a single unit.

There's a variety of different accessories you can purchase, depending on the size of your fryer. Cake and pizza plates, kabob skewers, and steamer adapters are only a couple of the available accessories I have used. A lot of recipe books are up for sale and online recipes are easy to find too.

## 4. Space Saver

You can enjoy this advantage if you have a small kitchen, or stay in a dorm room, or communal housing. Many of those units are around a coffee maker's size. They don't take up too much room on the counter and usually they're easy to store or move away.

I appreciate the fact that other appliances, such as a toaster oven, can be replaced and some people use them in kitchenettes or RVs that lack a proper oven. They're very handy to have breakroom in an office too!

## 5. Easy to use

Most fryers are really easy to use- just select the temperature and the cooking time, add food and shake a few times while cooking. No need to fuss or stir like using the stove top.

The baskets make shaking your food simple and fast as well, and the unit doesn't lose a lot of heat when you open it. So feel free to peek while cooking if you want! Unlike an oven, you won't be slowing things down if you do.

## 6. Ease of Clean Up

One part of cooking that most of us don't enjoy is the clean up. With an air fryer, you just have a basket and pan to clean, and many are even dishwasher safe. With non-stick coated parts, food usually isn't stuck to the pan and instead slides right off onto your plate. It takes just a few minutes to wash up after using. This inspires me to cook more frequently at home, so I don't care about cleaning up!

## 7. Energy Efficiency

These fryers are more efficient than using an oven, and they will also not heat up your house. I used mine during a heat wave and I love that when I'm using it, my kitchen isn't dry. If you're trying to keep your house cool throughout the summer, or worried about your electric bill, then you'll be amazed with how powerful these devices are.

# Breakfast recipes

## Air Fryer Donuts

INGREDIENTS
1/2 cup of granulated sucrose
1 tbs cinnamon
1 (16.3-ounce) Big flaccid biscuits, like Pillsbury Grands! Flaky Chips
Sprinkle with olive oil or coconut oil
4 spoonfuls of unsalted butter, melted

DIRECTIONS
Fill a parchment-papered baking sheet. In a small bowl , combine the sugar and cinnamon; set aside.
Remove the biscuits from the can, cut them apart and place them on the baking sheet. To cut holes out of the middle of each biscuit, using a 1-inch diameter biscuit cutter (or similarly shaped bottle cap).
Coat an air fryer basket gently with olive or coconut oil spray (do not use non-stick cooking spray such as Pam which can harm the basket cover).
In the air freyer, put 3 to 4 donuts in a single layer (they shouldn't touch). Cover the fryer to air and set to 350 ° F. Cook, flipping around halfway, before the golden-brown donuts, max 5 to 6 minutes. Place donuts onto the baking dish. Repeat with leftover biscuits. You should cook the donut holes too — they should take a minimum of around 3 minutes.
Brush with melted butter on both sides of the warm donuts, drop them in the cinnamon sugar and turn to cover on both sides. Serving wet.

## Cinnamon Banana Bread

Ingredients
Cooking spray
All-purpose 3/4-cup flour
1 Teaspoon cinnamon
1/2 teaspoon of kosher salt
Baking soda with 1/4 teaspoon
2 Mashed Bananas
2 Large, beaten eggs
1/2 tablespoon white sugar
Complete 1/4 cup Milk
2 Cups of palm oil
1/2 cubicle vanilla extract
2 Tablespoons of pickled walnuts

Directions

Preheat the fryer by air to 155 ° C (310 ° F). Coat a 6-inch round cake pan with a cooking spray at the bottom and sides.

In a cup, mix together the rice, cinnamon, salt and baking soda.

In a separate cup, add the pineapple, bacon, sugar, milk , butter, and vanilla extract. Fold banana mixture into flour mixture when mixed with batter; put into prepared cake pan. Sprinkle over batter with walnuts.

Place pan in the air fryer basket and cook for about 30 minutes, until a toothpick comes out clean when inserted in the middle.

Move the bread to a wire rack for 15 minutes to cool in pan. Take the bread off the pan to serve.

**Cheese Frittata**

Ingredients:
Eggs Start
Cheese cheddar
Mushrooms
Grape tomatoes (Tomatoes with cherry)
Spinach (chopped)
Freshly chopped herbs
Onion
Salt

Directions:
Preheat the fryer before 350 F/180 C.
Fill a 7-inch deep baking sheet with parchment paper, then grease and set aside.
Whisk the eggs together and the milk in a mug.
Apply salt to the cup, the remaining ingredients including the sea salt flakes, and whisk to mix.
Pour the frittata mixture into the baking saucepan and place it inside the basket of the air fryer.
Cook for 12-16 minutes, or before you placed the eggs. Place a toothpick inside the air fryer frittata core to search. When it comes out clean the eggs are ready.

## Healthy Pop Tarts

Ingredients
1 (15 oz) kg refrigerated pie crusts
6 tablespoons strawberry jam / preserves
2 cups white sugar
2-4 tablespoons heavy cream
2 tablespoons melted butter
1 teaspoon vanilla extract
Sprinkles

Instructions
Use a pizza cutter to cut each crust into 4 equal-sized rectangles. Combine the remaining flour, re-roll it out, and then make 4 more rectangles. You'll have 12 complete rectangles.
Place 1 tablespoon of strawberry jam in the center of 6 rectangles.
Spread the jam out to within 1/4 inch of the edge.
Use your finger to moisten the outside of each pie crust round with water.
Cover each filling rectangle with another pastry rectangle.
Press the seams together using your fingers, then use a fork to crimp the edges together.
Use a knife for poking up a few slits.
Click on the air fryer to "ON." Then press "PRE-HEAT" Set the heat to 350 degrees F and set the timer to 11 minutes. Tick "START."
When it's done preheating, the air fryer will beep at you. Open the air fryer and pour cooking spray into the pot. Place in basket two of the pop tarts. Close the fryer.
When it is finished cooking it will beep at you. Repeat with still pop tarts. Before frosting, Cool completely. During 5-10 minutes I threw mine in the freezer.
Whisk the powdered sugar, heavy cream , butter, and vanilla extract together in a small bowl, until well mixed.
Place frosting on the cooled tarts, then scatter with sprinkles.
Until serving cause frosting to harden in the fridge.

## Breakfast Bombs

Ingredients

Three slices of center cut bacon
3 Large, lightly beaten eggs
1 1/3 ounce fat cream cheese, melted
1 Table litre of fresh chives
4 Ounces of new pizza dough filled with whole wheat
Cooking spray

Directions

Cook the bacon over mild to very crisp in a small skillet, around 10 minutes. Remove bacon off the pan; crumble. Add eggs to bacon drippings in pan; cook for about 1 minute, stirring frequently, until almost firm, but still loose. Move eggs to a bowl; add cream cheese, chives and crumbled bacon to compare.

Divide the dough into four pieces equal to each. Roll each piece into a 5-inch circle onto a lightly floured surface. Place one-fourth of each dough circle in the center of the egg mixture. Brush the outside layer of the dough with water; wrap the dough around the mixture of the eggs to form a bag, pinch the dough at the seams together. In air fryer tray, put dough bags in a single layer; coat well with cooking spray. Cook for 5 to 6 minutes at 350 ° F until golden brown, then test for 4 minutes.

**Fried vegetables**
INGREDIENTS
Cooking spray
1 Cup panko crumbs with bread
1/4 cup Parmesan grated
1 TB. Seasoning Creole
2 Cups of blooming cauliflower
2 Cups of broccoli blossoms
1/2 whole cup of wheat flour
2 big Eggs
1 TB. Fresh, finely chopped parsley, optional
Marinara sauce, optional to serve
Direction
Air fryer preheat to 400 ° F.
Sprinkle the fryer bucket with grease, gently.
Combine panko, Parmesan, and criollo seasoning in a wide pot. Deposit back.
Place the flour and set aside in a shallow bowl. Whisk 2 eggs in a different bowl, then set aside.
Working in small lots, dip the cauliflower and broccoli into flour and shake off excess gently. Dip into the potato, then press the mixture into the breadcrumb. Place the florets in the basket, and cook for about 5-6 minutes until golden and crispy. Remove the basket from the fryer, and sprinkle with the parsley.
Serve with marinara sauce right away.

**Tasty Baked Eggs**
4 Yeasts
1 Lb of baby spinach, 7 ounces of ham torn, chopped
4 Tabletons of milk
1 Tablespoon of olive oil Spray
Salt and black chili, to taste
Directions:
1. Heat up a pan over medium heat with the oil, add baby spinach, stir cook for a few minutes and take off heat.
2. Grease 4 spray-cooking ramekins and split baby spinach and ham into each.
3. Crack an egg in each ramekin, divide the milk, season with salt and pepper, place ramekins at 350 degrees F in preheated air fryer and bake for 20 minutes.
4. For breakfast serve baked eggs.

## Breakfast Egg Bowls

Ingredients
4 Dinner wraps, tops left off, and scooped out inside
4 Heavy cream spoons
4 egg
4 Tablespoons mixed parsley and chives
Salt and black pepper, to taste
4 Parmesan spoons, rubberised
Directions:
1. Arrange dinner rolls on a baking sheet and each crack an egg.
2. Divide the heavy cream, combine the herbs with salt and pepper in each roll and season.
2. Sprinkle the parmesan on top of the rolls, bring them in the air fryer and cook for 20 minutes at 350 degrees F.
4. Divide the bread bowls into plates and serve breakfast. Enjoy it!

## Delicious Breakfast Soufflé

4 whisked eggs
4 Heavy cream spoons
A pinch of red, crushed chili pepper
2 persley spoons, chopped
2 Spoonfuls of chives, chopped
Salt and black pepper, to taste
Directions:
1. Mix the eggs with salt , pepper, heavy cream, red chili pepper, parsley and chives in a pot, whisk well and split into 4 dishes of soufflé.
2. Arrange dishes in the air fryer and cook the soufflés for 8 minutes at 350 degrees F.
2. Serve warm.

## Air Fried Sandwich

2 Half English muffins
2 Eggs
2 Strips of Bacon
Salt and black pepper, to taste
Directions:
1. Crack the eggs in the air fryer, put bacon on top, cover and cook for 6 minutes at 392 degrees F.
2. In your microwave, heat up your English muffin halves for a few seconds, split eggs into 2 parts, place bacon on top, season with salt and pepper, cover with the other 2 English muffins and serve for breakfast.

**Rustic Breakfast**

Ingredients
Baby Spinach 7 ounces
8 Mushrooms with chestnuts, halved
8 Onions, half sliced
1 Clove of garlic, minced
Four Chipolates
Four slices of bacon, chopped
Salt and black pepper, to taste
4 eggs
Cooking spray
Directions:
1. Grease the oil over a frying pan and add onions, garlic and mushrooms.
2. Add bacon and chipolatas, and finish with spinach and crack eggs.
2. Season with salt and pepper, put the pan into your air fryer's cooking basket and cook at 350 degrees F for 13 minutes.
4. Serve for breakfast and divide between plates.

## Bacon Wrapped Filet Mignon

Ingredients
2 Steaks with mignon filet
2 Bacon Strips
2 tootpick
1 Newly crushed tablespoon of peppercorns, we use a number of peppercorns
1/2 teaspoon of kosher salt
Apricot oil
Directions
Place the bacon around the mignon filet and cover it with a toothpick by pressing the toothpick through the bacon and into the filet, then to the bacon on the other end of the toothpick from the filet.
Season the steak with the salt and pepper or the seasonings you prefer.
Place the mignon filet covered with bacon on the air fryer shelf.
Sprinkle a small amount of avocado oil on the steak.
How long to cook filet mignon wrapped with bacon
Air fried the steak at 375 degrees F for about 10 minutes, and then turn as one side is cool and seared while the other is not.
Fry air for another 5 minutes, or until the desired doneness is achieved. We are pursuing medium.

**Omni air fryer oreos**
INGREDIENTS
4 Premade bags of crescent roll dough
5 Cookies to Oreo
1 T he powdered sucre
DIRECTIONS
Preheat the fryer until 385
Spray oil on a tray or the air fryer bucket
Wrap each Oreo cookie in a triangle of crescent rolls. Trim the excess dough and set aside
Combine the extra bits of dough to enclose the 5th cookie
At 385 fry the surface for 6 minutes or until dark golden brown, going partly by
Pour in powdered sugar and drink wet.

# Air Fryer Lunch Recipes

## Chicken, Corn, Beans and Quinoa Casserole

Ingredients
1 Cup quinoa, cooked beforehand
3 Cups breast chicken, cooked and shredded
14 Ounces of black canned beans
12 Corn Ounces
Chopped 1/2 cup cilantro
6 Kale buds, hammered
1/2 cup of green, chopped onions
1 Cup of tomato sauce, clean
1 Cup of new salsa
2 Tablespoons of chili powder
2 Cumin spoons, ground
3 Cups of mozzarella cheese, 1 spoonful of garlic powder Cooking spray
2 Chopped Jalapeno peppers
Directions:
1. Remove the quinoa, rice, black beans , peas, cilantro, kale, green onions, tomato sauce, salsa, chili powder , cumin, garlic powder, jalapenos and mozzarella, shake, place in your fryer and cook at 350 degrees F for 17 minutes.
2. Slice the lunch and serve warm.

## Chicken and Zucchini Lunch Mix

Ingredients
4 zucchinis, sliced with a spiralizer
1 Pound of chicken breasts, skinless, ostrich and cubed
2 Teaspoons of garlic, minced
1 Tablespoon of olive oil
Salt and green pepper, to taste
2 Cups of cherry tomatoes, half diminished
1/2 cup of chopped almonds
To the pesto:
2 Herb tassels
Kale, 2 cups, chopped
1 tbs Lemon juice
1 Clove of garlic
3/4 Cup Nuts
Olive oil 1/2 cup
A tablespoon of salt
Directions:
1. Mix basil with kale, lemon juice, garlic, pine nuts, butter and a touch of salt in your food processor, pulse very well and set aside.
2. Heat a saucepan over medium heat that fits your air fryer with the oil, add the garlic, stir and cook for 1 minute.
3. Add chicken, salt, pepper, stir, almonds, zucchini noodles, garlic, cherry tomatoes and the pesto you made at the beginning, stir gently, insert into preheated air fryer and cook for 17 minutes at 360 degrees F.
4. Divide between dishes, and serve lunch.

## Chicken and Corn Casserole

Ingredients-Ingredients:
1 Cup of chicken stock
2 Spoonfuls of garlic powder
Salt and green pepper, to taste
6 ounces of coconut canned milk
1 and a half cups of black lentils
2 Lbs. of chicken breasts, skinless, neckless and 1/3 cup cilantro, chopped
3 Cups of Maize
3 Pockets of Spinach
3 Red, chopped onions
Directions:
1. Mix the stock with coconut milk, salt , pepper, garlic powder, chicken and lentils in a saucepan that suits your air fryer.
2. Remove the corn, green onions, cilantro and spinach, stir well, place in the air fryer and cook for 30 minutes at 350 degrees F.

## Easy Chicken Lunch

1 bunch of chopped kale
Salt and green pepper, to taste
1/4 Cup stock for chicken
1 cup, shredded chicken
3 Chopped carrots
1 cup of shiitake mushrooms, cut roughly
Directions:
1. Mix stock and kale in a blender, pulse a few times and pour into a saucepan that fits your air fryer.
2. Add the chicken, mushrooms, onions, salt and pepper to taste, shake, place in the air fryer and cook for 18 minutes at 350 degrees F.

## Salmon and Asparagus

1 Lb Asparagus, Cut
1 tbs of olive oil
A sweet slice of paprika
Salt and green pepper, to taste
A small bit of garlic powder
A pinch of cayenne chili
1 Red bell pepper, half-cut
Smoked salmon 4 ounces

Directions:

1. Place asparagus spears and bell pepper on a lined baking sheet that suits your air fryer, add salt, pepper, garlic powder, paprika, olive oil, cayenne pepper, swirl to cover, put in the fryer, cook for 8 minutes at 390 degrees F, turn and cook for another 8 minutes.
2. Add salmon, cook for a further 5 minutes, split everything on plates and serve.

## Turkey Burgers

Ingredients-Ingredients:
1 Lb grounded turkey beef
1 Shallot, chopped
A splash of olive oil
1 Medium, chopped jalapeno pepper
2 tbs of lime juice
1 lime zest, grated
Salt and green pepper, to taste
1 Teaspoon, ground cumin
1 Teaspoon of sweet Guacamole paprika to eat

Directions:
1. Combine turkey meat with salt , pepper, cumin, paprika, shallot, jalapeno, lime juice and zest in a cup, stir well, shape burgers from this blend, drizzle the oil over them, put in preheated air fryer and cook at 370 degrees F per side for 8 minutes.
2. Divide between plates and top over with guacamole.

## Coconut and Chicken Casserole

Ingredients
4 Lime leaves cut
1 Cup Vegetable stock
1 Split stalk of lemongrass, 1 inch piece
Cut into thin strips 1 pound of chicken breast, skinless, boneless
Chopped 8 ounces of mushrooms
4 Thai Chilies, Split
4 Spoonfuls of fish sauce
6 oz coconut milk
1/4 tablespoon juice
Chopped 1/4 cup cilantro
Salt and green pepper, to taste

Directions:
1. Put stock in a saucepan that suits your air fryer, put over medium heat to a simmer, add lemongrass, ginger and lime leaves, mix and cook 10 minutes.
2. Strain soup, return to saucepan, add chicken, mushrooms, cheese, chilies, fish sauce, lime juice, cilantro, salt and pepper, stir, place in the air fryer and cook for 15 minutes at 360 degrees F.
3. Divide, and serve, into bowls.

## Zucchini Casserole

Ingredients
1 Cup Vegetable stock
2 tbs. of olive oil
2 Sweet, peeled potatoes and cut into medium wedges
8 zucchinis, cut into medium wedges
2 Bright, diced onions
One cup of coconut milk
Salt and pepper, to taste
1 tbs of soy sauce
1/4 tsp, dry thyme
1/4 Rosemary Teaspoon, Dry
4 Dill spoons, chopped
Chopped 1/2 teaspoon basil
Directions:
1. Heat a saucepan over medium heat that fits your air fryer with the oil, add onion, stir and cook for 2 minutes.
2. Add the zucchinis, thyme, rosemary, basil, potatoes, salt, pepper, stock, milk, soy sauce and dill, stir, put in your air fryer, cook for 14 minutes at 360 degrees F, split into plates and serve immediately.

## Sweet Potato Lunch Casserole

3 Large sweet potatoes squeezed with a fork
1 Cup Stock of Chicken
Salt and pepper, to taste
A pinch of cayenne chili
Nutmeg 1/4 teaspoon, ground
1/3 cup milk of coconut

Directions:
1. Place sweet potatoes in your air fryer, cook them for 40 minutes at 350 degrees F, cool them down, peel, chop roughly and transfer them to a saucepan that fits in with your air fryer.
2. Add the stock, salt , pepper, cayenne and coconut cream, toss, put in the air fryer and cook for 10 minutes at 360 degrees F.
3. Divide the casserole and serve into cups.

**Air Fried Thai Salad**

Ingredients-Ingredients:
1 Cup of carrots, rubberised
1 Cup red chicken, shredded
A tablespoon of black pepper and salt
A handful, chopped cilantro
1 Small, chopped cucumber
1 lime Juice
2 Red Curry Paste Teaspoons
12 Large, cooked shrimp, peeled and deveined

Directions:
1. Mix cabbage with carrots, cucumber and shrimp in a pan that fits your, toss, put in your air fryer and cook for 5 minutes at 360 degrees F.
2. Stir in salt , pepper, cilantro, lime juice and red curry paste, mix again, break between plates and serve immediately.

## Special Lunch Seafood Stew

Ingredients
5 Untitled White Rice
2 Untitled Peas
1 Chopped red bell pepper
14 Untitled White Wine
3 Units of water
2 Ounce bits of squid
Mussels 7 ounces
Sea bass filet 3 ounces, skinless, boneless and chopped
six scallops
3.5 Clams on ounces
4 shrimps
four cray fish
Salt and pepper, to taste
1 tbs of olive oil
Directions:
1. Mix the sea bass with crabs, mustels, scallops, crayfish, clams and squid in the pan of your air fryer.
2. Add the oil, salt and pepper, then toss to cover.
3. Mix salt, pepper, bell pepper and rice in a pot, then whisk.
4. Attach this over fish, add whine and water as well, put pan in your air fryer and cook for 20 minutes at 400 degrees F, stirring in half.
5. Break into bowls, and serve.

## Bacon Pudding

Ingredients
4 Strips of pork, fried and sliced
1 tbs butter, mild
2 Cups of Maize
1 Yellow onion, Split
Celery: 1/4 cup, chopped
Chopped 1/2 cup red bell pepper
Chopped 1 teaspoon of thyme
2 Teaspoons of ginger, minced
Salt and green pepper, to taste
1/2 cup milk, hard
1 1/2 cups of milk
3 Whisked shells
3 Cups of bread, filled
4 Parmesan spoons, rubberised
Cooking spray

Directions:
1. Grease the pan with coking spray on your air fryer.
2. Mix bacon with butter, broccoli, tomato, bell pepper, celery, thyme, garlic, salt , pepper, sugar, heavy cream, eggs and bread cubes in a bowl and scatter over the meat.
3. Apply this at 320 degrees to the preheated air fryer, and cook for 30 minutes.
4. Divide between plates, and serve warm for a quick lunch.

## Meatballs Sandwich

Ingredients
3 baguettes, cut more than halfway through
14 ounces steak, cooked
7 ounces tomato sauce
1 medium onion, chopped
1 shell, whisked
1 tablespoon bread crumbs
2 tablespoons cheddar cheese, grated
1 teaspoon oregano, chopped
1 litre of olive oil
Salt and green pepper, to taste
1 teaspoon thyme, dried
1 tablespoon basil, dry

Directions:
1. Combine meat with salt , pepper, onion, breadcrumbs, potato, cheese, oregano, thyme and basil in a cup, whisk, form medium-sized meatballs and add them to the air fryer after the oil has grated.
2. Cook them for 12 minutes at 375 degrees F, turning them in two.
3. Connect the tomato sauce, cook the meatballs for another 10 minutes and put on thin baguettes.
4. Immediately, serve

**Beef Stew**

Ingredients
2 Lbs. of beef, sliced into medium chunks
2 Chopped carrots
4 Chopped potatoes
Salt and pepper, to taste
1 qzt Vegetable stock
1/2 Smoked Paprika Teaspoon
A handful, chopped thyme
Directions:
1. Mix beef with carrots , potatoes, stock, salt , pepper, paprika and thyme in a dish that suits your air fryer, stir, put it in the air fryer basket and cook for 20 minutes at 375 degrees F.
2. Divide into cups, then eat lunch promptly.

## Cheese Ravioli and Marinara Sauce

Ingredients:
20 Ounces Ravioli cheese
Sauce with 10 ounces marinara
1 tbs of olive oil
1 Buttermilk in cup
2 Cups of minced bread
Parmesan: 1/4 cup

Directions:
1. Place buttermilk in a cup, then placed breadcrumbs in a dish.
2. Dip ravioli into buttermilk, then breadcrumbs, then put them on a baking sheet in your air fryer.
3. Drizzle olive oil over them, roast for 5 minutes at 400 degrees F, break them on plates, sprinkle parmesan on top and serve for lunch

## Turkey Cakes

Ingredients
6 Chestnuts, minced
1 tbs of garlic powder
1 tbs of onion powder
Salt and pepper, to taste
1 and 1/4 lbs turkey, ground
Cooking spray
Tomato sauce to serve

Directions:
1. Combine the mushrooms with salt and pepper in your mixer, pulsate well and move to a pot.
2. Instead of this blend add turkey, onion powder, garlic powder, salt and pepper, stir and form cakes.
3. Sprinkle them with a cooking mist, move to your air fryer and cook for 10 minutes at 320 degrees F.
4. Serve them side by side with tomato sauce and a savory side salad.

## Lunch Pork and Potatoes
Ingredients
2 Lbs. of pork
Salt and pepper, to taste
2 Red potatoes, sliced to medium quarters
1/2 Teaspoon crushed garlic
1/2 tablespoon of red chili flakes
1 Teaspoon of dried parsley
A splash of balsamic vinegar
Directions:
1. Mix the pork with carrots, salt , pepper, garlic powder, pepper flakes, parsley and vinegar in your air fryer oven, mix and cook for 25 minutes at 390 degrees F.
2. Cut pork, break on plates and potatoes and prepare for lunch.

## Creamy Chicken Stew
Ingredients
1 and 1/2 cups of celery cream
6 Tenders for Chicken
Salt and green pepper, to taste
2 Chopped potatoes
1 bay leaf
1 Spring thyme, chopped
1 tbs of milk
1 Yolk of an Egg
1/2 cup creame, hard
Directions:
1. Mix the chicken with celery sauce, carrots, heavy cream, bay leaf, thyme, salt and pepper in a cup, mix, pour into the pan of your air fryer and cook for 25 minutes at 320 degrees F.
2. Leave the stew to cool down a little, remove the bay leaf, split between plates and serve immediately.

## Italian Eggplant Sandwich

Ingredients
1 eggplant, Cut
2 dried parsley
Salt and pepper, to taste
1/2 cup of minced bread
1/2 tbs Italian seasoning
1/2 Teaspoon crushed garlic
1/2 Tablespoon dried onion
2 tbs of milk
4 Slices of bread:
Cooking spray
Mayonnaise: 1/2 cup
Sauce with 3/4 cup tomatoes
2 Cups of mozzarella, grated cheese
Directions:
1. Season eggplant slices with salt and pepper, put on for 10 minutes and dry well.
2. In a bowl , mix and stir in parsley and breadcrumbs, Italian seasoning, onion and garlic powder, salt and black pepper.
3. Mix the milk and mayo in another tub, and whisk well.
4. Rub the eggplant slices with the mayo paste, dip them in the breadcrumbs, put them in the basket of your air fryer, spray with the cooking oil and cook for 15 minutes at 400 degrees F, flip them after 8 minutes.
5. Brush with olive oil every slice of bread and place 2 onto a working sheet.
6. Add mozzarella and parmesan on each, add slices of baked eggplant, spread tomato sauce and basil and top with other slices of bread, grated side down.
7. Divide the sandwiches into plates, halve them and serve for lunch.

## Succulent Lunch Turkey Breast

Ingredients
1 Big turkey breast
2 Teaspoons of olive oil
1/2 Smoked Paprika Teaspoon
1 Teaspoon, dried thyme
1/2 tbs Sage Powder, dried
Salt and pepper, to taste
2 Mustard spoons
1/2 cup of maple syrup
1 tbs butter, mild
Directions:
1. Brush the turkey breast with the olive oil, sauté with salt, pepper, thyme, paprika and sage, powder, put in the basket of your air fryer and fry for 25 minutes at 350 degrees F.
2. Turn the turkey, cook for another 10 minutes, turn over again and roast for another 10 minutes.
3. Alternatively, fire up a skillet over medium heat with the butter, add mustard and maple syrup, mix well, simmer for a few minutes and take off oil.
4. Break the turkey breast, split it between plates and serve on top with the maple glaze drizzled.

## Steaks and Cabbage

Ingredients

Sirloin beef, 1/2 pound sliced into strips
2 Cornstarch Teaspoons
1 tbs of peanut oil
2 Cups of chopped cabbage
1 Yellow minced bell pepper
2 Green Onions, Sliced
2 Teaspoons of garlic, minced
Salt and pepper, to taste

Directions:

1. Mix the cabbage with the salt , pepper and peanut oil in a pot, toss, transfer to the basket of air fryer, cook for 4 minutes at 370 degrees F and transfer to a cup.
2. Fill your air fryer with steak strips, add green onions, bell pepper, garlic, salt , and pepper, mix and cook for 5 minutes.
3. Remove the cabbage, shake, break into plates and prepare for lunch.

## Stuffed Meatballs

Ingredients
1/3 cup of crumbs of bread
3 tbs of milk
1 tbs ketchup
1 egg
1/2 Marjoram Teaspoon, dry
Salt and pepper, to taste
1 lb of lean beef, ground
20 cubes of cheddar cheese
1 tbs of olive oil

Directions:
1. Mix the crumbs of bread with the ketchup, butter, marjoram, salt, pepper and egg in a bowl and whisk well.
2. With this mix add the beef, stir and shape 20 meatballs.
3. Form each meatball around a slab of cheese, drizzle the oil over it and polish.
4. Place the meatballs in your preheated air fryer and cook for 10 minutes at 390 degrees F.
5. Serve them with a side salad for lunch.

## Meatballs and Tomato Sauce

Ingredients
1 lbs of lean beef, ground
3 green, diced onions
2 Teaspoons of garlic, minced
1 Yolk of an Egg
1/4 Cup Crumbs of bread
Salt and pepper, to taste
1 tbs of olive oil
16 oz Tomatoes sauce
2 Mustard spoons
Directions:
1. Combine beef with onion, garlic, egg yolk, bread crumbs, salt and pepper in a cup, stir well and shape medium-sized meatballs from this combine.
2. Grease the meatballs with the grease, place them in your air fryer and cook them for 10 minutes at 400 degrees F.
3. Mix the tomato sauce with the mustard in a pot, shake, pour over meatballs, swirl and simmer for 5 minutes at 400 degrees F.
4. On plates split meatballs and sauce and prepare for lunch.

## Sweet and Sour Sausage Mix

Ingredients
1 Lb sausages, diced
1 Red pepper clove, sliced into strips
1/2 cup yellow, minced onion
3 Tablespoons of brunette sugar
Cup 1/3 Ketchup
2 Mustard spoons
2 Spoonfuls of apple cider vinegar
1/2 Cup Stock of Chicken
Directions:
1. Add sugar and ketchup, mustard, stock and vinegar in a tub, then whisk well.
2. Mix the sausage slices with bell pepper, tomato, and sweet and sour mixture in your air fryer oven, swirl and sear for 10 minutes at 350 degrees F.
3. Break into bowls, and eat tea.

## Bacon and Garlic Pizzas

Ingredients
4 Rolls for dinner, frozen
4 Hazelled garlic cloves
1/2 teaspoon dried oregano
1/2 Teaspoon crushed garlic
1 Cup sauce with tomatoes
8 Slices of bacon, cooked and peeled
1 and 1/4 cup cheddar cheese, ground together
Cooking spray
Directions:
1. Place dinner rolls on a working surface and click to get 4 ovals.
2. Sprinkle each oval with a cooking mist, move it to your air fryer and cook for 2 minutes at 370 degrees F.
3. Pour the tomato sauce on each oval, split the garlic, scatter with the oregano and garlic powder, bacon and cheese on top.
4. Return the pizzas to your heated air fryer and cook for another 8 minutes at 370 degrees F.
5. Serve them moist at lunchtime.

**Corn Casserole**
Ingredients
2 Cups of Maize
3 tbs of flour
1 egg.
1/4 Cup dairy
1/2 cup cream light
1/2 cup of Swiss cheese, rinded
2 tbs of butter
Salt and pepper, to taste
Cooking spray
Directions:
1. Mix the corn and starch, sugar , milk, light cream, cheese, salt , pepper and butter in a cup, then mix well.
2. Grease the tray of your air fryer with a cooking spray, pour in cream mixture, spread and cook for 15 minutes at 320 degrees F.
3. For lunch serve warm.

## Lunch Potato Salad

Ingredients:
2 Lb red potatoes, half exposed
2 tbs. of olive oil
Salt and pepper, to taste
2 Green Onions, Sliced
1 Chopped red bell pepper
Lemon juice: 1/3 cup
3 Mustard spoons

Directions:
1. Mix the potatoes with half of the olive oil, salt and pepper on your air fryer basket and sear for 25 minutes at 350 degrees F, rotating the fryer once.
2. Mix the onions and bell pepper and roasted potatoes in a bowl and shake.
3. Mix lemon juice with the remaining oil and mustard in a little cup, then whisk very good.
4. Attach this to salad with onions, mix well and eat for lunch.

## Lentils Fritters

Ingredients:
1 Cup of yellow lentils, 1 hour drenched and drained in water
1 Hot pepper chilli, chopped
1 inch slice of ginger, grated
1/2 cubit turmeric powder
1 Masala Garam Teaspoon
1 Teaspoon powder for baking
Salt and pepper, to taste
2 tbs of olive oil
1/3 cup of water
Chopped 1/2 cup cilantro
Spinach 1 and 1/2 cup, chopped
Four cloves of garlic, minced
Red onion: 3/4 cup, chopped
Chutney with mint to drink

Directions:
1. Combine lentils with chili pepper, ginger, turmeric, garam masala, baking powder, salt, pepper, olive oil, water, cilantro, spinach, onion and garlic in your blender, blend well and form small balls from this mixture.
2. Place them all at 400 degrees F in your preheated air fryer, and cook for 10 minutes.
3. Serve the meal of your veggie fritters and a side salad.

## Prosciutto Sandwich

Ingredients
2 Slices of Bread
2 Slices of a mozzarella
2 Sliced tomatoes
2 Slices of a prosciutto
2 Leaves of basil
1 tbs of olive oil
A pinch of black pepper and salt

Directions:
1. Arrange the mozzarella on a slice of bread and prosciutto.
2. Season with salt and pepper, put in an air fryer and cook for 5 minutes at 400 degrees F.
3. Drizzle the oil over the prosciutto, add the tomato and basil, cover with the other slice of bread, cut in half the sandwich and serve.

## Japanese Chicken Mix

Ingredients
2 Thighs of chicken, skinless and boneless
2 Slices of ginger, diced
Four cloves of garlic, minced
Soy sauce: 1/4 cup
Cup 1/4 Mirin
Sake 1/8 cup
1/2 tbs sesame oil
1/8 cup of water
2 tbs of sugar
1 spoonful of corn starch mixed with 2 spoonfuls of water
Sesame seeds to serve
Directions:
1. Place the chicken thighs in a bowl with ginger , garlic, soy sauce, mirin, sake, salt, water , sugar and cornstarch, swirl well, move to preheated air fryer and cook for 8 minutes at 360 degrees F.
2. Divide between bowls, scatter the sesame seeds on top and serve lunch with a side salad.

## Easy Hot Dogs

Ingredients
2 buns hot dogs
2 hot dogs
1 tbs Dijon Mustard
2 Tablespoons of cheddar cheese, rubberized
Directions:
1. Put the hot dogs in preheated air fryer and cook them for 5 minutes at 390 degrees F.
2. Divide hot dogs into hot dog buns, spread the mustard and cheese, return all to your air fryer and cook at 390 degrees F for 2 minutes more.
3. Serve in lunchtime

## Delicious Chicken Wings

Ingredients
3 lb Chicken Wings
One and a half cup Butter
1 Tablespoon of old seasoning in the bay
3/4 Cup Starch Potato
1 Lemon juice Teaspoon
Lemon wedges to serve
Directions:
1. Mix starch and old bay seasoning with chicken wings in a bowl, and toss well.
2. Place the chicken wings in the basket of your air-fryer and cook them for 35 minutes at 360 degrees F, shaking the fryer periodically.
3. Increase the temperature to 400 degrees F, cook the chicken wings for another 10 minutes, and break them into pieces.
4. Heat up a saucepan at medium heat, add butter and melt.
5. Attach the lemon juice, mix well, heat up, and drizzle over the wings of chicken.
6. Serve them with lemon wedges to the side for lunch.

## Beef Lunch Meatballs

Ingredients
1/2 pound of ground meat
1/2 pound minced Italian sausage
1/2 tbs crushed garlic
1/2 tbs ground onion
Salt and pepper, to taste
1/2 cup of cheddar cheese, rinded
Mashed potatoes, to serve
Directions:
1. Mix beef with sausage, garlic powder , onion powder, salt , pepper and cheese in a cup, stir well and shape 16 meatballs from this mixture.
2. Place the meatballs in your air fryer and cook for 15 minutes at 370 degrees F.
3. Serve the meatballs on the side with some mashed potatoes.

## Chinese Pork Lunch Mix

Ingredients
2 Eggs
2 Lbs. of pork, cut into medium cubes
1 Cup Maize Starch
1 tbs of sesame oil
Salt and pepper, to taste
A mix of five chinese spices
3 spoonfuls of canola oil
Sweet tomato-sauce to serve
Directions:
1. Mix 5 spices in a bowl with salt, pepper and cornstarch, then stir.
2. Mix the eggs with the sesame oil in another dish, then whisk well.
3. Dredge the pork cubes in a cornstarch mixture, then mix in the eggs and put them in the air fryer that you grated with the canola oil.
4. Cook at 340 degrees F, rotating the fryer once, for 12 minutes.
5. Serve pork with the sweet tomato sauce on the side, for lunch.

## Chicken Kabobs

Ingredients
3 Orange peppers, chopped in squares
1/4 Cup honey
One-third cup soy sauce
Salt and pepper, to taste
Cooking spray
6 mushrooms, half cut
2 Chicken breasts, skinless, ossified and loosely cubed
Directions:
1. Mix chicken with salt, pepper, honey in a pot, tell sauce and some cooking spray, then mix good.
2. String chicken, bell peppers and mushrooms on skewers, throw them into your air fryer and cook for 20 minutes at 338 degrees F.
3. Divide into glasses, and eat lunch.

## Turkish Koftas

Ingredients
1 Leek, Cut
2 Spoons of feta cheese, crumbled
1/2 pound of lean beef, slimming
1 tbs of grounded cumin
1 tbs of mint, chopped
1 tbs of parsley, chopped
1 tbs of garlic, diced
Salt and pepper, to taste

Directions:
1. Mix beef and leek, cheese, cumin, basil, parsley, garlic, salt and pepper in a pot, mix well, shape your koftas, and place them on sticks.
2. Attach koftas at 360 degrees F to your preheated air fryer, and cook for 15 minutes.
3. Serve them for lunch, with a side salad.

## Tasty Cheeseburgers

Ingredients
12 Ounces of lean, ground beef
4 Ketchup teapoons
Three tbs of yellow onion, chopped
2 Mustard Teaspoons
Salt and green pepper, to taste
Four slices of cheddar cheese
2 Half burger buns,

Directions:
1. Mix the beef with the onion, ketchup, mustard, salt and pepper in a bowl, stir well and form 4 patties out of the mixture.
2. Divide cheese into 2 patties and cover with the other 2 patties.
3. Place them at 370 degrees F in preheated air fryer, and fry them for 20 minutes.
4. Divide cheeseburger into 2 half buns, top with the other 2 and serve lunch.

## Philadelphia Chicken Lunch

Ingredients
1 tbs of olive oil
1 Cut, yellow onion
2 Skinless, boneless and diced chicken breasts
Salt and pepper, to taste
1 spoonful of Worcestershire sauce
14 Ounces dough of Pizza
1 and 1/2 cup cheddar cheese
1/2 Cup Cheese jarred sauce

Directions:
1. Preheat your air fryer to 400 degrees F, add half of the oil and onions, fry them for 8 minutes and stir once.
2. Add pieces of chicken, Worcestershire sauce, salt and pepper, toss, air fry for an additional 8 minutes, stir once and transfer everything to a bowl.
3. On a working surface, roll the pizza dough and form a rectangle.
4. Spread half of the cheese all over, add the mixture of chicken and onion, and finish with the sauce.
5. Roll the dough up and turn it into a U.
6. Place the roll in the basket of your air fryer, brush with the remaining oil and cook for 12 minutes at 370 degrees, turning the roll halfway through.
7. When it's nice break the roll and eat for lunch.

## Pasta Salad

Ingredients
1 Zucchini, half-sliced and about chopped
1 Orange bell pepper, sliced finely
1 Green, finely chopped bell pepper
1 Red onion, sliced roughly
4 Ounces of brown mushrooms, half
Salt and black pepper to taste
1 Italian Seasoning Teaspoon
1 pound of penne rigate, cooked already
1 Container of cherry tomatoes, half
1/2 cup of olive kalamata, pitted and half cut
Olive oil: 1/4 cup
3 Spoonfuls of Balsamic Vinegar
2 Table cubits of basil, minced

Directions:
1. Mix the zucchini with the mushrooms, orange pepper bell pepper, green bell pepper, red onion, salt , pepper, Italian seasoning and oil in a bowl, toss well, transfer to 380 degrees F preheated air fryer and cook for 12 minutes.
2. Mix pasta and cooked vegetables, cherry tomatoes, olives, vinegar and basil in a large salad bowl, then mix and serve for lunch.

## Delicious Beef Cubes

Ingredients
1 Lbs. sirloin, cubed
16 Jarred pasta sauce
1 and 1/2 cups crumbs of bread
2 tbs. of olive oil
1/2 Marjoram Teaspoon, dried
White rice, prepared already to eat

Directions:
1. Mix the cubes of beef with pasta sauce in a pot, then mix properly.
2. Mix the bread crumbs with marjoram and oil in another bowl, and stir well.
3. In this mix, dip the beef cubes, put them in your air fryer and cook for 12 minutes at 360 degrees F.
4. Divide between bowls, and serve side by side with white rice.

## Hash Brown Toasts

Ingredients.
4 Patty brown burger, frozen
1 tbs of olive oil
Cherry tomatoes: 1/4 cup, chopped
3 Mozzarella spoons, shredded,
2 Parmesan spoonfull, grated
1 tbs of balsamic vinegar
1 tbs, chopped basil

Directions:
1. Place the hash brown patties in the air fryer, drizzle the oil over them and cook them for 7 minutes at 400 degrees F.
2. Mix tomatoes and mozzarella, parmesan, vinegar and basil in a pot, then mix well.
3. Divide hash brown patties on plates, blend and serve for lunch, cover each with tomatoes.

## Fish And Chips

Ingredients
2 Small filets of cod, skinless and osseous
Salt and pepper, to taste
1/4 Buttermilk in cup
3 Cups kettle, fried chips

Directions:
1. Mix the fish with salt, pepper and buttermilk in a bowl, toss for 5 minutes and leave aside.
2. Put chips and crush them in your food processor and spread them on a plate.
3. At all sides add fish and press well.
4. Switch fish to the basket of your air fryer, and cook for 12 minutes at 400 degrees F.
5. For lunch serve hot.

## Lunch Chicken Salad

Ingredients
2 Corn ears, hulled,
1 pound of chicken, boneless
Olive oil according to need
Salt and pepper, to taste
1 cup of sweet paprika
1/2 tbs brown sugar
1/2 tbs crushed garlic
1/2 Lettuce iceberg head, cut into medium strips
1/2 Lettuce roman head, cut into medium strips
1 Cup of canned, drained black beans
1 Cup cheddar, ground cheese
Cilantro: 3 cubes, chopped
4 green, chopped onions
12 Sliced cherry tomatoes
1/4 cup dressing in ranch
3 tbs BBQ sauce

Directions:
1. Put the corn in the air fryer, drizzle some oil, mix, cook for 10 minutes at 400 degrees F, move it to a plate and set it aside for now.
2. Place the chicken in the basket of your air fryer, add salt , pepper, brown sugar, paprika and garlic powder, toss, drizzle some more oil, cook for 10 minutes at 400 degrees F, turn them halfway, move tender to a cutting board and chop.
3. Add chicken, iceberg lettuce, roman lettuce, black beans, cheese, cilantro, tomatoes , onions, bbq sauce and ranch dressing, stir well and serve for lunch.

## Lunch Fajitas

1 Cup of garlic powder
Cumin: 1/4 teaspoon, ground
1/2 tbs of chili powder
Salt and pepper, to taste
1/4 Tablespoon cilantro, field
Chicken breasts 1 pound, cut into strips
1 Sliced red bell pepper
1 Cut green bell pepper
1 Yellow onion, Sliced
1 tbs of lime juice
Cooking spray
4 Tortillas, Salsa warmed to serve
Sour cream, to serve
1 Cup of lettuce leaves, torn to serve

Directions:
1. Mix chicken with garlic powder, cumin, chili, salt , pepper, coriander, lime juice, red bell pepper, green bell pepper and onion in a cup, toss, set aside for 10 minutes, move to your air fryer and sprinkle some cooking spray throughout.
2. Toss and cook for 10 minutes, at 400 degrees F.
3. Arrange tortillas on a working board, break the chicken mix, add sauce, sour cream and lettuce, seal them and serve for lunch.

## Macaroni and Cheese

Ingredients
1 and 1/2 cups favorite macaroni
cooking spray
1/2 cup milk, hard
1 Cup Stock of Chicken
3/4 Cup cheddar, ground cheese
1/2 cup mozzarella, ground cheese
Shredded, 1/4 cup parmesan
Salt and pepper, to taste
Directions:
1. Sprinkle a casserole with a cooking spray, add macaroni, heavy cream, stock, cheddar cheese, mozzarella and parmesan but also salt and pepper, mix well, put casserole in the basket of your air fryer and cook for 30 min.
2. Divide into glasses, and eat lunch.

**Chicken Pie**

Ingredients
2 Thighs of chicken, ossified, skinless and cubed
1 Carrot, Cut
1 Yellow onion, Split
2 Chopped potatoes
2 Mushrooms, Split
1 tbs soy sauce
Salt and pepper, to taste
1 Italian Seasoning Teaspoon
1/2 Tablespoon crushed garlic
1 Worcestershire Teaspoon Sauce
1 Spoonful of flour
1 tbs of milk
2 Puff sheets of pastry
1 Mezzanine chocolate, melted

Directions:
1. Heat up a saucepan over medium high heat, add potatoes, carrots and onion, stir and cook for 2 min.
2. Add the chicken and mushrooms, the salt, the soy sauce, the pepper, the Italian seasoning, the garlic powder, the Worcestershire sauce, the flour and the milk.
3. Place 1 puff pastry sheet on the bottom of the pan and trim excess edge of your air fryer.
4. Attach the chicken mix, cover with the other layer of puff pastry, cut the excess and spray the pie with the sugar.
5. Place in an air fryer and cook for 6 minutes at 360 degrees F.
6. Leave the pie to cool, chop and eat for breakfast.

## Buttermilk Chicken

Ingredients
One and a half kilograms of chicken thighs
2 Buttermilk Cups
Salt and pepper, to taste
A pinch of cayenne chili
2 cups of white flour
1 Table litre of baking powder
1 spoonful of paprika
1 tbs of garlic powder
Directions:
1. Mix the chicken thighs in a bowl with buttermilk, salt , pepper and cayenne, toss and leave for 6 hours.
2. Mix the beef with the paprika, baking powder and garlic powder and cook in a separate dish,
3. Drain the chicken thighs, dredge them in a flour mix, put them in your air fryer and cook for 8 minutes at 360 degrees F.
4. Flip parts of chicken, cook them for another 10 minutes, put on a plate and serve for lunch

## Hot Bacon Sandwiches

Ingredients
1/3 cup sauce in bbq
2 Cups of honey
Eight slices of bacon, fried and divided into thirds
1 Sliced red bell pepper
1 Sliced, yellow bell pepper
3 Pita pockets sliced in half
Lettuce leaves 1 and 1/4 cup Butter, torn
2 Tomatoes, with slices

Directions:
1. Mix sauce bbq with honey in a pot, then whisk well.
2. Brush the bacon with some of this mixture and all the bell peppers, put them in your air fryer and cook for 4 minutes at 350 degrees F
3. Shake the fryer, then cook for another 2 minutes.
4. Stuff pita pockets with bacon blend, tomato and lettuce stuff, scatter the rest of the bbq sauce and serve for lunch.

## Fresh Chicken Mix

Ingredients
2 Skinless, boneless and cubed chicken breasts
8 mushrooms, Cut
1 Chopped red bell pepper
1 tbs of olive oil
1/2 Teaspoon, dried thyme
10 ounce alfredo sauce
Six slices of bread
2 tbs butter, soft

Directions:
1. Mix chicken with mushrooms, bell pepper and oil in your air fryer, toss well to coat, and cook for 15 minutes at 350 degrees F.
2. Transfer the chicken mixture to a bowl, add the thyme and alfredo sauce, toss, return to air fryer and cook for another 4 minutes at 350 degrees F.
3. Spread the butter on slices of bread, add the butter side up to the fryer and cook for another 4 minutes.
4. Arrange toasted slices of bread on a platter, cover each with a variation of chicken and serve for lunch.

## Chicken Sandwiches

Ingredients
2 Skinless, boneless and cubed chicken breasts
1 Red onion, Cut
1 Sliced red bell pepper
Italian Seasoning for 1/2 cup
1/2 Teaspoon, dried thyme
2 Cups of lettuce with butter, torn
4 Pita
1 cup of cherry tomatoes
Half a tbs of olive oil

Directions:
1. Mix chicken with onion, bell pepper, Italian seasoning and oil in your air fryer, then mix and cook for 10 minutes at 380 degrees F.
2. Transfer the mixture of chicken to a pot, add the thyme, butter lettuce and cherry tomatoes, swirl well, fill the pita pockets with this combination and serve for lunch.

## Scallops and Dill

Ingredients
1 Lb Sea Scallops
1 Lemon juice tbs.
1 Teaspoon dill, shredded
2 tbs of olive oil
Salt and green pepper, to taste
Directions:
1. Mix the scallops with dill, sugar, salt, pepper and lemon juice in your air fryer, cover and cook for 5 minutes at 360 degrees F.
2. Dispose of unopened ones, split scallops and dill sauce on plates and serve as lunch.

## Lunch Special Pancake

Ingredients:
1 tbs of butter
3 Whisked eggs
1/2 Cup of flour
1/2 Cup of milk
1 cup of Salsa
1 Cup of thin, peeled and deveined shrimp
Directions:
1. Preheat the air fryer to 400 degrees F, add the fryer plate, add 1 spoonful of butter and melt.
2. Combine the eggs with flour and milk in a cup, mix well, spill into the air fryer pan, scatter, cook for 12 minutes at 350 degrees, and move to a tray.
3. Mix shrimp and salsa in a bowl, stir and serve your pancake sideways with this.

## Lunch Shrimp Croquettes

Shrimp: 2/3 pound, fried, peeled, deveined, chopped
1 and 1/2 cups crumbs of bread
1 Whisked Egg
2 Lemon juice c.l.
3 Red, chopped onions
1/2 Teaspoon, dried basil
Salt and green pepper, to taste
2 Lbs. of olive oil
Directions:
1. Mix half the bread crumbs in a bowl with the egg and lemon juice, then stir well.
2. Remove the green onions, basil, salt, pepper and shrimp, then mix properly.
3. Mix the remainder of the bread crumbs with the oil in a separate dish, then mix well.
4. Shape the round balls out of a mixture of shrimp, dredge them in bread crumbs, put them in preheated air fryer and cook them at 400 degrees F for 8 minutes.
5. Serve them with a lunchtime dip.

# Poultry recipes

## Chicken and Rice

INGREDIENTS

3 Cups (325 g) cold rice
1 Cup (130 g) leftover, cubed chicken
5 Tbsp of soy sauce tamari or usual, if not gluten free
1.5 Cup frozen vegetables (I used peas and sweet corn)
2 Cut green onions (spring onions),
1 Tsp of the sesame oil
1 Tsp fuel oil
1 Tbsp available chili sauce
Salt

Directions

The air fryer is preheated to 350F/180C.
In a large pot, mix all the ingredients together.
Then move to a non-stick pan which fits within the basket of the air fryer.
Cook for 20 minutes, stirring a few times before heating the rice mixture.

## Chicken wings

Ingredients

Non-stick spray, for basket
2 Lbs. of chicken wings, cut at the joint and drop tips
Salt
4 Spoons of unsalted butter
1/2 cup chili sauce, like the RedHot Frank's
Ranch dressing or blue cheese, to serve

Directions

Spray the bowl with the cooking spray of a 3.5-quarter air fryer and put aside. Pat the dry chicken wings, then brush with salt generously. Place the wings in the fryer basket so that they do not strike (the drumettes standing upright along the sides if necessary to fit in). Set the air fryer to 360 degrees F, cook for 12 minutes, then turn the wings with tongs and cook for another 12 minutes. Flip the wings again, lift heat to 390 degrees F and cook until extra-crispy on the outsides, about 6 minutes more. In the microwave, heat the butter up in a microwave-safe bowl until cooled, around 1 minute. Whisk in the sauce, sweet.

Place the wings in a wide bowl with the butter mixture to cover and serve with side sauce.

## Rotisserie chicken

Ingredients
Full chicken
Salt
Freshly ground spicy chili
2 T of preferred oil like olive oil or avocado oil (I use avocado oil spray)
1 T Dried thyme
1 tbs Seasoning Italian
2 tbs of garlic powder
2 tbs of onion powder
1 tbs of paprika

DIRECTIONS

Wash the chicken and truss it, tying the legs, wings and thighs.

Insert the chicken over the spit of the rotisserie. Skip the move if using a regular air fryer.

The thyme, Italian seasoning, garlic powder, onion powder, and paprika combine in a small bowl.

Sprinkle with oil and salt or rub the chicken, and pepper to taste.

Rub the chicken into the seasoning mix.

Put the chicken inside the air fryer.

Air fried or roast for an hour at 380, or before the chicken reaches an internal temperature of 160-165 degrees.

Cut the chicken, and allow it to rest for 10 minutes under a foil tent.

## Tasty Chicken Tandoori

Resources

1 pound (453.59 g) of tendered chicken, cut in half each
1/4 cup (50 g) Greek Full-Fat Yogurt
1 Tablespoon Powdered Ginger (1 tablespoon)
1 Tablespoon of minced garlic (1 tablespoon)
1/4 cup (4 g) of cilantro
1 Teaspoon Cosher Salt (1 teaspoon)
1/2 â€ "Cayenne Pepper 1 Teaspoon
1 Teaspoon Turmeric (1 teaspoon)
Garam Masala 1 Teaspoon (1 Teaspoon)
1 Teaspoon (1 teaspoon) Smoked paprika, add to the chicken a smoky flavour, and color

For Total

1 Table cubit (1 shelf cubit) Oil or ghee.
2 Teaspoons (2 teaspoons) Juice Lime, to finish
2 Tablespoons (2 tablespoons) of chopped coriander, to be garnished

Directions

Mix all ingredients in a glass bowl except the basting oil , lemon juice and 2 cilantro spoonfuls. 30 Seconds to Marinate.
Open the air fryer and place the tandoori chicken carefully in a single layer either on the rack or in the air fryer bowl.
Baste the chicken with either oil or ghee on one hand, using a silicone cloth.
Cook for 10 minutes, at 350F.
Drop and loop over the chicken and throw to the other leg,
Cook 5 more minutes.
Test to see if the internal temperature has exceeded 165F using a beef thermometre. Don't miss this step.
Place on a serving plate and remove. Sprinkle with cilantro and apply the lemon juice to blend properly.

## Thyme turkey breast

INGREDIENTS

1 5 lb Turkey Breast, meat on bone
4 cups of unsalted butter
2 Tbsp Chopped Fresh Sage
1 Tbsp Seasoning Poultry
2 Tsp Salt at Sea
1 Tsp Black Potatoes
1 Tsp Garlic Powder

DIRECTIONS

TO BUTTER HERBS:

Let 4 spoons of butter arrive at room temperature so that it is soft enough to mix herbs and seasonings.

Place butter in a small bowl and add salt, pepper, garlic powder and freshly chopped sage to season with poultry.

Mix until fully combined. This is rubbed under the skin and on top of the skin to make the turkey breast flavor.

AIR FRYING TURKEY:

Remove the defrosted turkey breast from the fridge and let it sit on the counter for about 15-20 minutes at room temperature to take off the chill. It will keep the meat from being captured and being too heavy.

Remove the turkey breast from the package and pat until completely dry with paper towels. Cut any extra skin from the neck section, with kitchen shears.

Lift the skin and spread the mixture of herbal butter under the fat, over the fat and over the remainder of the turkey breast until fully coated,

Remove turkey breast side down to air fryer basket breast and place a sheet of foil on top to avoid burning. Make sure the turkey breast fits completely in the air fryer without the top heat factor being touched.

Switch on 350 air fryer and cook for 30 minutes. Using tongs, flip turkey breast after 30 minutes, so that the meat side is up and place the foil on top of the breast. Cook for another 20 minutes.

Remove the foil and cook for another 10 minutes, or until the skin is browned to look desired.

Using tongs, remove the entire turkey breast from the air fryer, and put 10-15 minutes before cutting and serving onto a plate and covering with foil.

## Caribbean chicken

INGREDIENTS
3 lbs boneless, skinless thigh chicken fillets
Ground black pepper
Salt
1 Tbsp of ground seed coriander
1 Tbsp of cinnamon ground
1 Tbsp cayenne chili pepper
1-1/2 tsp terrestrial ginger
Nutmeg ground 1-1/2 tsps
Coconut oil, 3 tbsps, melted

DIRECTIONS
Take chicken off the packaging and pat dry. To soak up any remaining moisture, put on a large baking sheet covered with paper towels. Chicken is salted and peppered on both sides. Let the chicken stay for 30 minutes, so before going into the air fryer, it's not so cold.

Combine the coriander, cinnamon, cayenne, ginger and nutmeg in a shallow pot. Cover with spice mixture each piece of chicken, then spray with coconut oil on both sides.

Place four pieces of chicken in your air fryer basket (they shouldn't overlap but if they touch it's okay). Air to cook for 10 minutes at 390 degrees F. Remove the chicken from the basket and place the chicken in a safe oven dish, tightly covered with foil. Hold the chicken warm in the oven before it is cooked. Repeat the directions for frying air with the rest of the chicken

## Turkey Meatballs

Resources
1 pound ground turkey
1/2 cup Bread crumbs with panko
1 egg.
1/4 cup fresh parsley
1 tbs low sodium soy sauce
Black pepper
Directions
Blend ingredients into a pot.
Sprinkle the air fryer basket gently, and place half of the meatballs in the bowl.
Cook meatballs for 5 minutes, at 400 degrees. Switch over the meatballs, and simmer for another five minutes.
Remove cooked meatballs and place, and repeat, the remaining uncooked meatballs in the air fryer basket. Heat at 400 degrees for 5 minutes, turn over and simmer for another 5 minutes.

## Buttered turkey wings

INGREDIENTS
2 Lbs Turkish Wings
3 spoonfuls of olive oil or sesame oil
3 to 4 spoonfuls of chicken rub (see my recipe suggestion)
DIRECTIONS
Place the turkey wings in a large mixing pot.
Then fill in the bowl with the olive oil or sesame oil and add some rub.
Using your hands to spread the rub over the turkey wings.
Then place the turkey wings in the basket of an air fryer, place the basket in the air fryer.
Set the 380 degrees F, or 180 degrees C. Just flip the wings with tongs after 13 minutes.
Set it for another 13 minutes, when the time is up.
Drop the turkey legs, platter and drink from the air fryer.

# Beef and Lamb recipes

## Lamb chops
Resources
Chops 8 far lambs 1 1/4 "long
2 Mustard, dijon or whole grain spoons 2
1/2 cubit olive oil
1 Teaspoon of tarragon, (any herb dried by your choice)
1 Lemon juice tbs.
Salt and chilli
Directions
Switch air fryer on to preheat to 390 °.
Layer mustard, olive oil, tarragon and lemon juice in a small bowl, then blend well.
Rinse with a paper towel, then pat dry lamb chops.
Mixture of mustard paste on all sides of lamb chops.
Put lamb chops in a bowl with some space in between. You should do them in loads and put them on a table covered in plastic wrap until they are all done. Instead, place them in a 225 ° oven and keep them warm.
For medium rare (turning at 8 minutes) cook for 15 minutes. You don't have to turn them on but I like the even color it provides from rotating them around.
To test for doneness, you can use a thermometer. The diameter of the chop used can change the cooking times. When you don't have a thermometer, I use a knife to cut into one to test.

## Roast beef
INGREDIENTS
2.5 Lb Beef Roast (can go up to 4 lb)
1 Spoonful of Olive Oil
Seasoning to taste (I used seasoning on Montreal Steak)
DIRECTIONS
Join the roast and it's more lightweight
Fry the bbq with olive oil
Add seasoning according to need
Place the roast on the rotisserie or tray or in the basket of the air fryer
Air fried on medium rare beef at 360 for about 15 minutes per pound.
Allow to cook for 5 minutes and serve

## Seasoned beef roast

Resources

2 Lbs of roast beef
1 tbs of olive oil
1 Onion, medium (optional)
1 teaspoon salt
2 Tsp thyme and rosemary, (fresh or dried)

Directions

Preheat air fryer to 200 ° C (390 ° F).

On a platter, combine sea salt, rosemary and oil.

Pat the beef with paper towels and roast dry. Put beef roast on a plate and change to cover the outside of the beef with the oil-herb mixture. Seasoned beef served on a white platter

Drop the roast beef into the bowl of the air fryer.

Peel and cut the onion in half, if used. In the air fryer basket. Beef roast in air fryer basket, place onion halves next to the beef

Set to cook for 15 minutes at air fryer.

Switch temperature to 360 ° F (180 ° C) when the time is up. Some air-fryers require you to turn food while cooking, so check your manual and turn over the beef roast if necessary (my Philips Viva airfryer doesn't need to turn food).

Put the beef on for another 30 minutes to cook. This will give you beef of medium-rare origin. Using a meat thermometer is better to track the temperature and ensure it is cooked and your taste. Cook for a further 5 minute interval if you want it to be cooked more well.

Take the roast beef from the air fryer, cover with foil in the oven, and leave to rest for at least 10 minutes. This helps the meat to finish frying, and reabsorb the juices into the skin.

Carve the roast beef against the grain thinly and serve with grilled or steamed potatoes, mustard wholegrain, and gravy.

## Filet mignon

**INGREDIENTS**
2 Steaks with mignon filet
Olive oil spray, or extra virgin olive oil light coating
Salt and chilli

**DIRECTIONS**
For cooking filets in the air fryer, start by spraying with avocado oil on each side of the steak, and each side is generously salted and peppered.
Next, put the filets in your basket or grill plate if you are equipped with one of the air fryers. I like cooking stuff like steak on a wire rack with a sheet pan underneath with the air fryer model I use, the Breville Smart Oven Air, to keep the drippings from making a mess ... it's definitely not important though.
Preheat your refrigerator to 375 ° F. Place in fryer in the air and cook for 10 minutes on the first leg. Flip the filets and cook for another 5 minutes, or until the preferred doneness hits the steak.
Drop the air fryer filets, cover with foil and let rest 10 minutes before eating.

## Artichoke pepper beef

**INGREDIENTS**
2 Small sized artichoke
1 Small Lemon, just juice
Olive oil 1 spoonful
1 Salt Tablespoon
Black Chili on taste

**DIRECTIONS**
Preheat the air fryer to 340 ° Fahrenheit (170 ° Celsius)-it is enough for 4-5 minutes. Under cold water clean the artichokes. Remove the leaves outside (about 7-10), cut the ends, and shorten the stem. Split them lengthwise, in two. Turn them until you face the cut leg.
Pour over a generous quantity of fresh lemon juice (roughly 1/4 lemon per piece). Attach olive oil and season with salt and pepper to taste. Now put them cut side down and repeat in preheated air fryer (drizzle with olive oil and season with salt and pepper).
Cook at 340 ° Fahrenheit (170 ° Celsius) for 12-15 minutes (or until ready).
Serve with your preferred dip.

## Air fryer beef meatballs

Resources
One pound of ground beef
1 pound of pork
1 Big peeled onion, roughly chopped
4 Minced garlic cloves
1/4 cup of roughly chopped parsley
2 Lightly beaten eggs
1/2 cup Italian breadcrumbs, seasoned
1/2 cup crumbled cheese with feta
1 Tbsp Sauce with Worchestire
1 teaspoon salt
1/2 tsp black chilli

Directions
In a mini food processor, mix onion, garlic cloves and parsley to shape. Process through until finely chopped. Deposit aside.
Layer the ground beef, bacon, onion mixture, eggs, breadcrumbs, Italian seasoning, feta cheese, Worchestire sauce, salt and black pepper in a big pot. Using hands to blend before blended.
Grab 2 Tbsp of meat mix and go into a ball. In all meatballs are rolled match with the meat mixture.
Place meatballs in single layer Air Fryer basket to ensure the meatballs are not touching. Place basket in Air Fryer and cook for 10-12 minutes at 400 degrees Fahrenheit, or until an internal temperature exceeds 165 degrees C.

## Cheese stuffed pork chops

Resources
1/2 tbs olive oil
1 Rib of celery, diced
1/4 cup of trimmed onio
4 White bread, cubed
2 Tablespoons of fresh parsley minced
1/8 Salt Teaspoon
1/8 Sage Rubbed Teaspoon
1/8 White pepper Teaspoon
1/8 tbs of dried marjoram
1/8 tbs of dried thyme
1/3 cup chicken broth with reduced sodium
CHOPS TO PORK:
4 Chops of pork ribs (7 ounces each)
1/4 tbs salt
1/4 tablespoon chili pepper

Directions

Heat up oil over medium-high heat in a large skillet. Add celery and onion; cook and stir for 4-5 minutes, until tender. Out of heat strip. Combine bread and seasonings in a large bowl. Remove the combination of the celery and the broth; swirl to paint. Deposit aside.

Cut a pocket in each chop of pork, almost to the bone, making a horizontal slice. Fill the chops with a mixture of bread; secure with toothpicks where appropriate. Preheat air-fryer to 325 degrees. Sprinkle with salt and pepper over chops. Arrange in single layer in air-fryer basket on greased plate. Cook on for 10 minutes. Turn and cook until 165 ° is read by a thermometer inserted into the stuffing center, and the thermometer inserted into pork reads at least 145 °, 6-8 minutes longer. Let stand for 5 minutes; remove the toothpicks before served.

## Olive feta beef

Resources
85 percent lean 1 lb ground beef
Crumbled 3/4-cup Feta cheese
1/4 cup crushed, diced green olives
1/2 cup of onion diced
2 Tbsp Sauce with Worcestershire
1/2 tsp Seasoning Montréal Steak
2 Dashes ground garlic
Salt

Directions
Combine all ingredients in a Medium Bowl. Form 4 Patties equal. Put the hamburgers in Air Fryer and cook the med or med rare on 400F for 15 min for well done or less.

## Lamb scallop casserole

Resources
8 Wide (1-oz.) sea scallops, very dry and washed and patted
1/4 tbs pepper
1/8 tbs Salt
Cooking spray
Extra virgin olive oil: 1/4 cup
2 Tablespoons of flat-leaf parsley, very finely chopped
2 Capers with teaspoons, very finely minced
1 Tablespoon of finely ripened lemon zest
1/2 cubicle of finely chopped garlic
Lemon wedge, optional

Directions
Sprinkle the scallops with salt and pepper. Coat an air fryer basket with spray for the cooking. Place the scallops in the basket and cover with spray for frying. Place the basket inside the fryer. Cook the scallops at 400 ° F for about 6 minutes, until they reach an internal temperature of 120 ° F.

In a small bowl , mix oil, parsley, capers, lemon zest, and garlic. Drizzle over the scallops. When needed serve with lemon wedges.

# Pork Recipes

## Seasoned pork loin

INGREDIENTS
Tenderloin pork (1.25lbs-1.75lbs)
2 tbs of brown sugar
1 tbs of smoked paprika
1 Tsp mustard
1/2 tsp powdered onion
1.5 tbs salt
1/2 tsp black pepper
1/4 tsp ground garlic
1/4 tsp (optional) cayenne powder
Olive oil: 1/2 tbs

DIRECTIONS
In a bowl, combine all the dry ingredients.
Trim any excess fat / silver skin into the pork tenderloin. Coat with 1/2 lb olive oil. Rub the combination of spices on whole pork tenderloin.
Preheat the fryer with air for 5 minutes to 400 ° F. Place pork tenderloin carefully into air fryer after 5 minutes, and fry food at 400 ° F for 20-22 minutes. The internal temperature will be 145 °-160 ° F.
When the air fryer process is complete, extract pork tenderloin carefully to a cutting board and require to rest 5 minutes before slicing. Save some juices over grilled beef for cooking.

## Glazed pork ribs

Resources
2 Pound pork ribs, country style
2 tbs veg oil
1/4 tbs of salt
1/4 tablespoon hot chili pepper
2 Tablespoons of olive oil
1 Shallot, thinly cut
1/3 Spoon sauce with chili
Preserves of 1/3 cup apricots
1 tbs, reduced soy sauce
1 tbs fresh ginger
1/8 Tea cubit crushed chipotle pepper
2 Tablespoons of fresh caught chives

Directions

Preheat an air fryer to 350 F (175 C). Oven preheat to 200 degrees F (95 degrees C). Brush 2 tablespoons of oil to the ribs and season with salt and pepper. In the air fryer bowl, position 1/2 of the ribs in a single row.

Fry in the preheated air fryer for 15 to 20 minutes, until ribs are fork-tender and thoroughly baked. A center-inserted instant-read thermometer will read 145 degrees F (63 degrees C). Move ribs to a baking pan, and put them in the preheated oven to keep the remaining ribs warm when cooking.

In the mean time, boil 2 teaspoons of oil over medium heat in a shallow saucepan. Add shallot; stir and cook for about 3 minutes, until tender. Stir in chili sauce, apricot preserves, soy sauce, chipotle pepper and ginger. Heat and stir for 3 to 5 minutes, until bubbly.

Transfer ribs onto a serving dish. Gently brush with glaze and garnish with chives

## Stuffed pork roll

Resources

2 Tablespoon Mustard Dijon
1 spoonful of apricot preserves
1.5 Fresh rosemary minced in a tablespoon or 1/2 tsp. Rosemary washed, and crushed
1.5 New thyme minced in a tablespoon or 1/2 tsp. Dry thyme
2 Garlic leaves, sliced
1 boneless loin roast pork (2 lbs.)
0.5 Salt Teaspoon
0.5 pepper Teaspoon
2 Fully cooked sausage andouille links (about 1/2 lb.)
6 Strips of Bacon
0.25 Tassel Chicken broth
0.25 tables White wine

Directions

1. Combine the first 5 ingredients into a small bowl. Deposit aside.
2. Develop a slit down the middle of the roast lengthwise to about 1/2 in. Bottom up. Open roast so it lays flat; cover with wrapping plastic. Slightly square. Plastic cover strip. Season with pepper and oil.
3. Set up 2 sausage links in roast centre. Close the roast; brush the mixture with mustard. Cover pork roast in. Keep kitchen string tied several times. Load wine and broth into the inner pot. Place roast with handles on the wire rack; lower onto the inside dish. Pressure lid to lock. Press the function pressure; select the setting for the pork. Set to cook medium (30 minutes). Beginning.
4. Naturally let pressure relax for 10 minutes; relieve any remaining pressure quickly. Fill with lid to fried the food. Press the fry function for air; select custom setting. Timer press; set to 10 minutes. Beginning. A pork-inserted thermometer should reach at least 145 °, and the bacon should be somewhat crisp. Let it stand before slicing for 5 minutes. Line erase.

## Herb butter pork chops

INGREDIENTS

4 Thin sliced bone-in pork chops (about 1.25 kg)
2 Teaspoons of new rosemary chopped
1/2 teaspoon of coarse salt at sea
3 spoonfuls of extra virgin olive oil
1/4 cup of fresh minced parsley
One Lemon Zest

INGREDIENTS

Season pork chops with salt and rosemary.
Put 2 chops in air fryer basket and cook for 10 minutes at 400-degrees F
The sauce is made while the pork is frying. Combine olive oil, parsley, lemon zest, citrus juice and salt in a small bowl. Mix properly, and put aside.
Using tongs to cut the pork chops when the cook time is finished, and pass them to a pan or serving platter. Repeat steps before 2 remaining chops are fried.
Spoon sauce over and eat grilled pork chops.

## Pork stew

Resources
1/2 cup Parmesan grated cheese
1 Tablespoon of paprika
1 Cup of garlic powder
1 Kosher salt
1 Tablespoon of dry parsely
1/2 cubic tablespoon black pepper
4 (5 ounces) pork chops with middle break
2 Spoonfuls of extra virgin olive oil

Directions
Preheat the air fryer to 380 F (190 C).
In a small , shallow dish, add Parmesan cheese, paprika, garlic powder, cinnamon, parsley, and pepper; blend well.
Cover with olive oil on each pork chop. Dredge in the Parmesan mixture on both sides of each chop and set on a tray.
Place 2 chops in the air fryer basket, and cook for 10 minutes; flip through cooking time halfway.
Switch to a cutting board, and require 5 minutes to relax. Undo with chops left over.

## Meatloaf

Resources
1 Cup of soft, fresh bread crumbs
1/4 cup broth for beef
1/2 cup sliced mushrooms
Shredded 1/2 cup carrots
1/2 cup of chopped onions
2 Garlic Cloves
2 Lightly beaten eggs
3 tbs Ketchup
1 Tbsp Mustard-style Dijon
1 Tbsp Sauce with Worcestershire
1/2 tablespoon kosher salt
2 lbs. Boiled beef
For Glazing
Cup 1/2 Ketchup
1/4 cup sugar
2 Tsp Mustard dijon

Directions

In a small bowl, add breadcrumbs and beef broth, and stir until the breadcrumbs are coated. Deposit aside.

Attach mushrooms, vegetables, garlic, onions and cycle until finely chopped. Place in big bowl.

In a large bowl, add ground beef, bacon, soaked breadcrumbs, ketchup, Dijon-style mustard, Worcestershire sauce and salt. Mix with hands until built-in. Forme in a sandwich.

Air Fryer is preheated to 390 degrees. *

Place the Meatloaf and cook for 40-45 minutes in Air Fryer.

When cooking meatloaf prepare glaze by mixing ketchup, brown sugar and mustard dijon. When you are left on your timer for about 5 minutes, spray glaze in Air Fryer over the meatloaf.

Remove the meatloaf and allow to rest 10 minutes before slicing.

### Cajun pork chops
Resources
4 Pork chops
1 Tablespoon of paprika
1/2 tbs of ground cumin
1/2 teaspoon black pepper
1/2 cayenne clove seasoning
1/2 cubit teaspoon of dried sage leaves
1/2 tablespoon of salted garlic
1 1/2 cups of extra virgin olive oil
Directions
Preheat the fryer until 400F
Mix the paprika, cumin, black pepper, cayenne pepper, sage, and garlic salt together in a bowl. Coat the spice mixture with each pork chop, be generous
Sprinkle a little oil over the chopped pork seasoning
Place the chops in the basket of the air fryer and cook for 8-10 minutes.

### .Jerk pork butt
Resources
1,5 lbs of pork ass chopped into 3 inch large pieces
Paste with 1/4 cup jerk
Basket Sprinkler Oil
Directions
Rub pork parts with jerk paste and require the pork to be marinated in the refrigerator for 4-24 hours. The better the longer.
Air fryer preheat to 390 degrees F. Spray the basket bottom to ensure it doesn't stick.
Drop pork and allow for a 20 minute rest at room temp. Place them in the air fryer to ensure spacing. Set 20 minutes to date, turn on halfway.
Remove from the air fryer and allow to sit before cutting for 5-10 minutes.
Pleasure.

## Pork sausage and peanut sauce

Resources

2 garlic leaves, crushed
2 tbs fresh ginger root, grated ginger powder or 1 tablespoon
2 Teaspoons of chili pepper paste or hot sauce
2-3 Tablespoons of soy sweet sauce
2 Cups of veg oil
400 g lean chops of pork, in 3 cm cubes
1 Shallot, thinly cut
1 tbs coriander
200 ml of coconut lactose
100 g of unsalted peanuts,

Directions

Mix half the garlic with the ginger in a dish, 1 teaspoon of hot pepper sauce, 1 tablespoon of soy sauce and 1 tablespoon oil. Mix together the meat and leave to marinate for 15 minutes.

AirFryer preheat to 200 ° C.

In the bowl, put the marinated meat and slip it into the AirFryer. Set the timer to 12 minutes, and roast until brown and done. Switch while you cook.

Meanwhile, make the peanut sauce: heat 1 tablespoon of oil in a casserole, and sauté the shallot gently with the rest of the garlic. Add the coriander and fry even more for a short period.

Mix with the shallot mixture the coconut milk and peanuts with 1 teaspoon hot pepper sauce and 1 tablespoon soy sauce and simmer gently for 5 minutes while stirring. Add a little water if necessary, if the sauce is too thick. Season with soy sauce, and mild pepper sauce to compare.

# Seafood and fish recipes

## Baked tilapia
Resources
4 fillets
1 Citrus
1 Tbsp Avocado oil (high-temperature oil) against sticking
1 Jane's First Mixed-up Salt, our Tilapia favorite
Directions
Brush Oil with Tilapia
Sprinkle your favorite seasonings with the fillets. (We want salt blended in)
Spray the air fryer basket with a non-stick cooking spray or spritz with frying oil
Air Fry the tilapia for 8-12 minutes at 400 ° F 205 ° C, rotating once.
Plate, and have fun!

## Baked shrimp scampi
INGREDIENTS
1 pound of big shrimp
8 tbs of butter
1 tbs minced garlic (use 2 for flavoring extra garlic)
1/4 c white wine or Sherry cooking
1/2 tbs of salt
1/4 tbs Cayenne Chili
1/4 tbs of paprika
1/2 tbs of onion powder
Bread crumbs 3/4 c
DIRECTIONS
Mix the brown crumbs and the dry seasonings in a dish
Melt the butter with the garlic and the white wine on the top of the stove (or in the Instant Pot on saute).
Cut from heat and add the shrimp and the crumb mixture
Transferr the mixture to a saucepan
Bake or fried with air at 350 for 10 minutes or until crispy
Serve, and have fun!

## Greek fish

**INGREDIENTS**
To the fish:
12 Ounces of boneless, skinless fillets of white fish such as cod, halibut, branzino
1 Teaspoon salt, split
1 tbs of all-purpose flour
1 Big egg, beaten
1/2 cup crumbs of panko
1/4 cup of garlic powder
1/4 spoonful of oregano
Sprinkle with olive oil
To the tacos:
1 tomato, chopped
1/4 cup red onion diced
3 Cups of white chopped cabbage
Fresh dill, on finish
8 Thin, warm flour tortillas (such as taco flour tortillas by mission street)
8 Lemon wedges
Tzatziki mint sauce:
Stonyfield basic 3/4 cup 0 percent Greek yogurt fat
1/3 cup grated cucumber, separated seeds and skin (from 1 medium)
1 Thin, crushed clove of garlic
1 Teaspoon of fresh juice of lemon
1/2 cup of healthy mint, minced
1/2 spoonful of new dill, chopped
1/4 + 1/8 tbs. kosher salt
Clean black chilli, to taste

**DIRECTIONS**
Place the cucumber with a package of cheese grater in a mini food processor or grate. Drain the liquid from the cucumber into a metal strainer and use a spoon back to help squeeze the excess liquid out.
Combine to eat with butter, ginger, lemon juice, basil, dill, salt, pepper and refrigerate.
Season 1/2 teaspoon salt for trout. Cut in 8 bands.
In a shallow bowl, place the flour on a plate, and the egg. Combine panko with the remaining 1/2 teaspoon salt, garlic powder and oregano on another tray.
The Process of Air Fryer:
Preheat the fryer by air to 400F. Cover the bits of fish in the starch, shake off the excess, then into the shell, then into the panko, then onto a parchment or wax paper lined sheet. Sprinkle with oil on both sides of the fish then transfer to the basket and cook for 4 minutes in a single layer, turn and cook for 2 to 3 more minutes, until golden and crisp.

## Tasty crab cakes

Resources
8 Once a lump crab
1/4 cup chopped red pepper
2 Chopped green onion
2 Octopus mayonnaise
2 Tbsp of bread crumbs
1 Tbsp Mustard dijon
Seasoning with 1 tsp old bay
Spraying oil
Lemon Squeeze

Directions
Layer red pepper bell, green onion, crumbs of toast, mayonnaise, mustard dijon and old bay in a bowl and stir until mixed.
With mixture, gently form 4 patties.
Place basket in Air Fryer and spray the tops lightly with oil.
Air fried for 10 minutes on 370 degrees Fahrenheit. Squeeze and open a little bit of lemon over the tops before serving.

## Simple salmon patties

INGREDIENTS
Fresh or canned salmon 14 ounces (400 g)
Chopped 3 tbsp cilantro (coriander)
3 Green Onions, finely mined (spring onions)
1 tbs of smoked paprika
1 egg.
Salt

DIRECTIONS
Preheat the fryer with air to 360 ° F/ 180 ° C.
Mince the fresh salmon or open the salmon tins, drain and remove the bones (if you prefer, you can leave in; I really like the bones). When using fresh salmon, extract by hand bones and slurry.
Remove all the ingredients and pour into a pot.
Form 6 patties, ensuring they are of the same size.
Stir in the air fryer bowl of patties and brush gently with no-calorie cooking oil.
Cook for 6-8 minutes, turning the patties through the cooking time over halfway.

## Avocado shrimp

Resources
1/2 cm. Raw peeled and deveined shrimps
1 1/2 tablespoon of avocado oil
1/4 tbs kosher salt
1/4 cup of chili pepper
1 tbs of sesame oil
2 minced garlic cloves
1 tbs ginger
2 Green onions, thinly diced, divided by white & green sections
3 Cups Cabbage Pre-sliced Mix
Chili garlic sauce 1/4 to 1/2 Tablespoon
2 tbs of soy sauce
8 Egg wrappers
California avocado sliced into eight slices
Sprinkle with olive or canola oil
Tasty chili sauce to serve
Baked on oven only:
1 egg.
2 tbs water

Directions

Chop the shrimp roughly, and place them in a bowl. Add 1/2 tsp of avocado oil, salt and pepper to taste.

Hot a medium-high-heat, non-stick skillet. Add the shrimp and cook for about 3 minutes, stirring occasionally, until just cooked through. Pass into a clean bowl. Wipe the pan clean with a paper towel.

In the pan boil up the remaining 1 teaspoon of avocado oil and sesame oil. Add the green onion with garlic, ginger, and white sections. Cook for 30 seconds, with stirring.

Stir in a mixture of cabbage. Cook, stirring frequently, for 3 to 4 minutes, until the cabbage wilts. Stir in green onion chili garlic sauce, soy sauce, and lime bits. Stir in the cooked shrimp and remove from heat.

Let filling cool down for about 10 minutes.

# Vegetarian Recipes

## Avocado fries

Resources
1/2 cup of all-purpose flour (about 2 1/8 oz.)
1 1/2 cups of black chili
2 big Eggs
1 tbs of water
1/2 cup panko (the breadcrumbs in Japanese style)
2 Avocados, cut together into eight wedges
Cooking spray
1/4 tbs kosher salt
1/4 cup ketchup with no extra spice
2 Teaspoons mayonnaise canola
1 spoonful of apple cider vinegar
1 Sriracha Chili Sauce 1 Tablespoon

Directions

In a small dish, mix the flour and pepper together. In a second, shallow dish, lightly beat the eggs and water. Place the panko in a shallow third platter. Dredge wedges of avocado in flour and shake off waste. Dip in a mixture of shells, causing the waste to trickle down. Dredge in panko and press to adhere. Avocado coat wedges well with spray for cooking.

Place avocado wedges in air fryer basket and cook for 7 to 8 minutes at 400 ° F until golden, turning the avocado wedges over halfway through frying. Remove from the frying pan; sprinkle with salt.

As avocado wedges cook, ketchup, mayonnaise, vinegar, and Sriracha are whisked together in a small bowl. To serve, place 4 avocado fries with 2 spoonfuls of sauce on each plate.

## Spinach bake

Ingredients:
Clean Spinach: 300 g
2 tbs butter
2 Tsp crushed garlic
Salt and Pepper

Directions

Rinse the spinach in a sieve underneath a cool press. Squeeze out gently some excess water so the spinach isn't too warm.

Place the spinach with your butter and seasonings in your air fryer cake pan and add to the end.

Set the temperature to 3 minutes and to 180c/360f.

Give it a short stir with a fork after it is beeps and then cook again for a final 2 minutes at the same temperature.

Relax and serve.

## Broccoli fritters

Resources
Skinless chicken thighs 1 pound, sliced into small pieces
2 Grand Eggs
1/2 tsp dried garlic
1/2 cup almond flour
1 cup of cheddar ground cheese
2 Cups of broccoli blossoms, steamed and finely chopped
Salt & pepper, to taste
Olive oil

Directions

Combine the bits of bite size chicken, garlic powder, bacon, almond flour, melted cheese, broccoli, salt and pepper in a big pot.

Combine gently.

## Air Fryer

The combination is scooped into a GREASED tub. Create fritters of standard size at your air fryer. The number of fritters depends on how big the air fryer is. Using a spoon back to flatten them out.

Set the air fryer to 400F and cook for eight minutes.

Flip over for another 2 minutes and cook.

If you do thicker fritters you need to increase the cooking time. Still test for doneness before you remove the fryer from air.

Repeat these moves until you have used up all of your "batter."

## Simple baked vegetables

Resources
1 Cup of broccoli blossoms
1 Cup of flowering cauliflower
1/2 cup carrots
1/2 cup yellow, sliced squash
1/2 cup, sliced baby zucchini
1/2 cup cut mushrooms
1 Little onion, in slices
Balsamic vinegar: 1/4 cup
1 tbs of olive oil
1 Tablespoon of chopped garlic
1 Teaspoon salt
1 Teaspoon of black chile
1 Teaspoon red flakes pepper
1/4 cup Parmesan cheese

Directions

Super easy and delicious air fryer roasted vegetables that can be made super fast for dinner in under 20 minutes! # Healthyrecipe # Healthyrecipes

Air Fryer pre-heat up for 3 minutes at 400.

Put olive oil, balsamic vinegar, garlic, salt and pepper flakes in a big pot, and red pepper.

Really easy and delicious roasted vegetables with air fryer that can be made super quick for dinner in under 20 minutes! # Healthyrecipe # Healthyrecipes

Whisk along.

Really simple and tasty roasted vegetables with air fryer that can be made really quick for dinner in under 20 minutes! # Healthyrecipe # Healthyrecipes

Add vegetables and coat with toss.

Really simple and tasty roasted vegetables with air fryer that can be made really quick for dinner in under 20 minutes! # Healthyrecipe # Healthyrecipes

Attach vegetables to bowl with Air Fryer. Cook on for eight minutes.

Shake vegetables, and cook for a further 6-8 minutes.

Attach the cheese and bake for one to two minutes

## Parmesan brussels sprouts

INGREDIENTS

1 pound Brussels sprouts, ends clipped and half longitudinally sliced
2 Tablespoon of olive oil
2 Tsp juice of lemon
3 Garlic leaves, minced
1/2 tbs of salt
1/2 cup parmesan grated cheese, divided

DIRECTIONS

Air fryer hot to 375 degrees.

Toss brussels sprouts, olive oil, lemon juice, garlic, salt and 1/4 cup of parmesan cheese together in a medium dish, then blend properly.

Place the brussels sprouts in a single layer of your air fryer bowl. Sprinkle with 1/4 cup of parmesan cheese and fry for 8 minutes, then shake the bowl.

Continue to air fry for another 7 to 8 minutes, or until the brussels are tender and crisp.

Delete from the air fryer, season with extra salt and parmesan cheese and enjoy!

## Stuffed tomatoes

Ingredients
4 Wide or 6-8 Small Tomatoes
1 teaspoon salt
1 TB. Ultra virgin oil
1/4 sweet, finely minced onion (1/4th cup)
1 Tsp garlic
1/2 lb. Good Italian sausage, without casings
1/4 hp. Organic chopped basil, with garnish
3/4 in. Bread crumbs of panko
1 Cup mozzarella grated cheese
1/4 hp. Parmesan Freshly Polished
Salt and pepper

Directions
Core tomatoes and 2" wide ring atop each tomato
Spray the tomatoes inside and sprinkle with salt to remove water
Place the tomatoes on a paper towel upside down and allow to drain while filling
Heat olive oil in a large skillet over medium to high heat. Attach the onion and garlic, and sauté for 1 to 2 minutes before fragrant. Remove sausage, break it with a wooden spoon, and cook for 8 minutes until browned and cooked through.
Add new basil, panko, mozzarella, and Parmesan to compare.
In air fryer, put the tomatoes and season inside with salt and pepper.
Stuff sausage tomatoes (filling will shrink when you roast, so make careful to stack tops until they appear like they're overflowing)
Jet fried for 10 minutes at 350 before the cheese melts and the tops become golden

# Snack and appetizer recipes

## Haddock nuggets

Resources
TO THE BREAD COD
1 1/2 pound of cabbage fillets sliced in 8 pieces
Season with salt and pepper
1/2 tablespoon flour
1 Tbsp ointment + 1 bath
1/2 cup cracker crumbs, or crumbs of cornflakes
1 Table litre of vegetable oil
TO THE HONEY TARTAR SAUCE LEMON
1/2 cup mayonnaise low in fat or no in fat
1 Honey Teaspoon
Half a lemon zest, finely minced
Half lemon juice
1/2 tsp Sauce with Worcestershire
1 Tbsp sweet savory pickle
Pinch black chilli

Directions

Crush crackers (or corn flakes) into small crumbs in a food processor, around a cup. Pulse the crumbs with 1 tbsp of vegetable oil.
Coat the chunks of cod with salt and pepper then dredge in the flour.
Next dip the chunks of flour dredged cod into the wash of the egg and finally into the crumbs of the cracker. Press the crumbs into all cod nugget surfaces to get sufficient coverage on both sides of the crumbs.
Preheat Airfryer by Philips to 180 degrees C. Place half of the cod nuggets in the basketplace plus use the rack to cook half at the top.
Set the timer within 15 minutes. Cut from basketball and enjoy with a garden salad or some fresh Airfryer French fries.

HONEY LEMON TARTAR SAUCE TO PREPARE

Simply mix well all the ingredients together and allow the flavors to blend before ready to serve to sit in the fridge.
For better flavor, you can even make this sauce day in advance.

## Herb Mushrooms

Resources
1 Lb Button or mushroom Crimini
1 to 2 Tbsp of oil
1/2 tsp sea salt
Italian seasoning: 1/4 tsp
2 Cloves of garlic, minced

Directions

Leave the small mushrooms entirely, cut the medium in half and cut the large into quarters.

Add the mushrooms and the oil, Italian seasoning, garlic, salt , and pepper to a medium-sized bowl. Stir to merge.

3-5 minutes to preheat the air fryer.

Based on the pattern, spread the mushrooms out in one sheet on the air fryer rack or in a jar.

Cook the roasted mushrooms in the air fryer for 6 minutes, then toss them or shake your bowl with air fryer.

Continue to cook them for another 5-6 + minutes before cooked completely.

Serve hot, with eggs or other vegetables, alongside a juicy steak, pork chops. Love it!

## Mashed Potatoes

Ingredients

4 Washed and dried sweet potatoes,
Olive oil: 3 tbsp
One and a half cup Butter
1/2 c milk 2% or whole, may want to thin out further

Directions

Clean potatoes, and thoroughly dry them. Prick up all the way around potato with a fork.

Apply gently with olive oil outside bodies, sprinkle salt on the outsides if you like at this moment. Can leave simple too, depending on the preferred taste.

Place the air fryer rack or basket on and schedule for 45 minutes to 400 degrees. Halfway into cooking time flip through.

Cut when the inside is tender (test with a knife placed in the middle of the largest potato) and allow to cool enough to hold it.

Remove the skins outside and place them inside a pot.

Add softened butter and beat with electric mixer at low, or combine well with potato masher. Add milk gradually, and any other seasonings you want.

Sweet potato mash with a slight amount of cinnamon and/or maple syrup is perfect.

## Cinnamon honey glazed sweet potato

INGREDIENTS

3 Medium / big soft potatoes
1 Tbsp Extra Virgin Olive Oil
2 Tbsp Raw Honey Where Possible
2 Cinnamon Tsp.

DIRECTIONS

Wash and cut sweet potatoes, then slice them into pieces.

Add the oil, honey, and cinnamon in a large mixing bowl and toss until evenly coated.

Attach sweet potatoes to the fryer gas, and cook for 20-25 minutes on 400. You will need to cut the sweet potatoes in two, and cook one batch at a time, depending on the size of your air fryer.

Crispy on the outside and fluffy on the inside would be sweet potatoes until finished. Remove the sweet potatoes from the air fryer and allow to rest for 5 minutes.

Serve, and have fun

**Creamy zucchini dip**

Ingredients
1 Minor Zucchini
Spanish bread crumbs and 1/4 cup seasoning
1/4 Cup flour
Your seasoning blend of choice
1 Egg + 2 teaspoons water, beaten
Olive oil spray pump (not aerosol!)

Directions
To cut the zucchini into thin "chips," using a mandolin slicer or a knife.
Prepare two small bowls to get the zucchini dredged. One cup will contain the pounded egg and one for the mixture of bread crumbs, seasonings and flour.
Dip each zucchini into the mixture of the eggs and dredge them in the bowl with flour and bread crumb. Shake off the excess and lie in your air fryer tray in a single layer.
Air to fry for 10 minutes at 375. Check about halfway through the process, as cooking time can vary depending on your zucchini's moisture content.

## Healthy carrot fries

INGREDIENTS

4 Carottes
1 Tsp Flour Corn
1 tsp Peppers
Garlic Powder 1/2 Tsp
Olive oil 1 Tsp.
Salt, just to taste

DIRECTIONS

Preheat your air fryer to 200C/390F using either the preheat mode, or run your air fryer at that temperature for 5 minutes.

Put all ingredients in a bowl, except for salt, and mix properly.

Place the carrots into the basket or tray of the air fryer, making sure they are in one layer and not moving. It helps them stay clean. If you have a smaller air fryer you may need to cook in batches.

Cook for 15-20 minutes, slicing through the carrots in half, until they are crisp on the outside and fluffy on the inside. You may need a taste test here but I'm sure there isn't going to be a question!

If needed, serve immediately with a sprinkle of salt on top and a hot dipping mayonnaise sauce.

## Artichoke dip

Ingredients
3 Cups Fresh Spinach Baby-Hacked
1 tbs Oil
8 Ounces Cheese Milk-Soft
1/4 Sour Cream
Mayonnaise Cup 1/4
1-2 Cloves of garlic-peeled, grated
1/2 cup of garlic powder
1/2 tbs Seasoning of dried Italian
1/4 cup of onion powder
Salt / Pepper-to taste (salt is easy)
1/2 Cup Artichoke Hearts Split Marinated
2 Cups Monterey Jack Cheese sliced (or mozzarella)-split
Chopped Parsley Clean

Directions
Heat the oil over medium heat in a sauté pan. Add fresh spinach, and cook until wilted spinach. (Approximately 5 minutes) Allow the spinach to cool for 5-10 minutes and then move to paper towels or a fine mesh strainer. Discard as much material as possible.

Combine cream cheese, sour cream, mayo, ginger, garlic powder, Italian season, onion powder, salt and pepper into large bowl. Use a hand mixer to create a smooth, fluffy base.

Add wild spinach, chopped artichokes and 1 cup of shredded cheese to try. Move the blend to a healthy 1 quarter oven tray.

Directly place the dip dish onto the air fryer basket. Water to cook for 5 minutes at 375oF.

Finish with 1 cup of shredded cheese.

Air fried 4-6 more minutes at 375oF, or until the surface is browned and bubbled. Sprinkle with chopped fresh parsley, and serve hot.

## Mix nuts

INGREDIENTS

1 Cup of almonds with nuts, cashews, hazelnuts, peanuts etc.

DIRECTIONS

Set the heat to 325 ° F.

Timings can vary based on the nuts used (Almonds-6 minutes, Peanuts, 10 minutes, Hazelnuts-6 minutes, and Cashew Nuts-8 minutes)

Be sure to throw the nuts for even browning at the halfway point.

Let the nuts cool down completely before storing them away from direct sunlight in a glass jar.

## Ranch chickpeas

Ingredients

1 15 ounce chickpeas can be drained, but not rinsed, then the moisture can be preserved!

1 Table litre of olive oil-split

4 tbs of dried dill

2 Spoonfuls of garlic powder

2 Cups of onion powder

Sea salt: 3/4 spoon

1 tbs Lemon juice

Directions

Toss the chickpeas and 1 teaspoon of the liquid you've saved from the can together in a medium pot. Air to fry for 12 minutes at 400 ° F.

Move the chickpeas back to your tiny bowl and mix in the olive oil, dill, garlic powder , onion powder, salt and lemon juice so that the beans are soft and powdered.

Switch the chickpeas back into your air fryer basket and cook for another 5 minutes at 350 ° F

Now eat, or fully cool and then put in an airtight jar

# Dessert recipes

## Carrot cake

INGREDIENTS
140 g Mild brown sugar
2 Eggs, whipped
Butter: 140 g
1 Lime, Garlic & Juice
200 g Flour to self-raising
1 clove of ground cinnamon
175 g rubbed carrot, (about 2 small carrots)
Sultanas: 60 g

DIRECTIONS
Preheat the fryer with air before 160C.
Cream the butter and the sugar together in a pot.
Remove the pounded shells, gently.
Fold in the flour, mix it up as you go, a little bit at a time. Attach the orange juice and zest, grated sultanas and carrots. Mix the ingredients softly together.
Grease the baked pan and pour in the mixture.
In the air-fryer basket, place the baking tin and cook for 30 minutes. Check and see if the cake has cooked-use a metal skewer or a cocktail stick to poke in the middle. If it springs wet then cook it a little longer.
Remove the baking tray from the airfryer basket and allow to cool before removing from the tray for 10 minutes.

## Pumpkin muffin

Ingredients
1 Cup of flour
1 Tsp of baking powder
1/3 Cups of sugar
Extract 1 Tsp Vanilla
1 Tbsp pumpkin powder
Puree with 1/3 Mix pumpkin
1 Egg
1/4 cup of milk
3 Tbs oil

Directions

Place the muffin liners into a tray of muffins. Deposit back.

The flour, baking powder and sugar are mixed in a dish. The vanilla extract, pumpkin spice, pumpkin puree, egg, milk and butter are mixed in another cup. Slowly blend in wet ingredients into dry ingredients, whipping until all is well blended and no lumps are left.

Heat the temperature to 360 degrees and fried air for 10 to 12 minutes. Split the batter between the muffin liners Put in the air fryer bowl.

## Banana Chocolate brownies

Ingredients
All-purpose 1/2 cup flour
6 Tbsp unsweetened raw cocoa
Cup sugar: 3/4
1/4 cup melted butter
2 big Eggs
1 Tbsp veg oil
Extract 1/2 tsp of Vanilla
1/4 tbs salt
1/4 teaspoon baking powder

Directions
Prepare your 7-inch baking pan by generously greasing on the bottom and on all sides with butter. Deposit back.
Preheat your Air Fryer by setting the temperature to 330 degrees Fahrenheit, allowing it to run for about 5 minutes while your brownie batter is being prepared.
In a large bowl , add the all-purpose flour, cocoa powder , sugar, butter , eggs, vegetable oil, vanilla extract, salt and baking powder and stir until thoroughly mixed. Add it to the baking pan prepared, and smooth it out.
Place in your preheated Air Fryer and bake 15 minutes or until mostly clean comes out a toothpick entered in the centre.
Remove from and allow to cool before removing and cutting in the pan.

## Blueberry cakes

INGREDIENTS
INTERVIEW:
2 Tables Baking Jiffy Mix
1 3/4 cup blueberry
14 Ounces condensed milk
1 Lemon zest in tablespoon
3/4 Cup Butter melted
Topping:
Jiffy Cake Mix: 1/2 cup
Brown sugar ½ cup
2 Molten butter spoons

DIRECTIONS

Start by combining all the ingredients in the cake into a big mixing bowl.
Blend well.
Spray the non-stick cooking spray on your air fryer protected pan.
Pour the batter into the healthy casserole air fryer (Note: this made 2 cakes)
Alternatively, combine the ingredients in the top into a small mixing pot.
Sprinkle the top over the cake layer.
Depending on how many fits into your air fryer basket, set your pan or pan and set the time at 320 degrees F for 10 minutes, check your cake after 10 minutes, and set it for another 5 minutes. Note: Use a toothpick because will air fryer is special to see if it comes out clean, if not add a few minutes, you want it fried all the way through.

## Sicilian cannoli

Ingredients
TO THE FILL:
1 (16-oz.) Ricotta container;
1/2 C. Cheese made with mascarpone
1/2 C. Divided, powdered sugar
1 C. C. Crème Heavy
THE SHELLS:
2 C. All-purpose flour, plus surface finish
1/4 c. Garnished sugar
1 Tps. salt
1/2 tbs. Cinnamon
Four cents. Cold butter, in cubes
INGREDIENTS

1 Tps. Extract pure Vanilla
1 Tps. Orange peel
1/4 tbs. salt
1/2 C. Small chocolate chips, garnishing

6 pcs. Blank wine
1 Big Egg
1 White potato, to clean
Vegetable oil, to fry

FILLING at MAKE:
Drain ricotta with a fine mesh strainer set above a large bowl. Let drain in the fridge for at least one hour and until overnight.
Beat heavy cream and 1/4 cup powdered sugar in a large bowl using a hand blender until stiff peaks develop.
Combine the ricotta, mascarpone and remaining 1/4 cup powdered sugar, cinnamon, orange zest and salt in another large bowl. Fold into milk with whipping. Refrigerate for at least 1 hour, before ready to fill with cannoli.
Create SHELLS WITH:
Whisk the rice, sugar , salt, and cinnamon together in a large bowl. Break the butter with your hands or pastry knife into a flour mixture until pea-sized. Add wine and milk, then combine until it forms a flour. Knead the dough in a tub a few times to help it come together. Pat in a flat disk, then seal in plastic wrap and refrigerate for a minimum of 1 hour and up to overnight.
Divide the dough into half on a lightly floured surface. Half spread out to 1/8 "wide. Use a cookie cutter with 4 "circle to cut dough out. Repeat with leftover dough. Re-roll scraps to carve out some more rings.
Wrap dough around cannoli molds and brush the whites of the eggs where the dough must touch to seal.
BY FRYER AIR:
Working in batches, place molds in air fryer basket and cook for 12 minutes at 350 °, or until golden.
Gently remove twist shells from molds when cold enough to treat or use a kitchen towel to stay on.
Place a pastry bag fitted with an open star tip to fill in. Filling the tubing into tubes, then dipping ends in small chocolate chips.

## Pear bread pudding

Ingredients
2 Ounces of semi-sweet, chopped chocolate
Half and a half cup crème
2/3 Cups of sugar
Two percent 1/2 cup milk
1 big egg, room temperature
1 Vanilla Teaspoon Extract
1/4 tbs salt
4 Day-old bread strips, crusts discarded and split into cubes (about 3 cups)
Optional toppings: sugar and whipped cream for the confectioners

Directions
Melt the chocolate in a small, microwave-safe bowl; mix until smooth. Stir in the cream; throw aside.
Whisk the sugar, milk , egg, vanilla and salt in a large bowl. Stir in dark chocolate. Attach pieces of crust, then flip to cover. Let them stand for 15 minutes.
Air fryer preheat to 325 °. Spoon 8-oz greased bread mixture into 2. Ramshawks. Place on tray in basket with air-fryer. Cook for 12-15 minutes before a knife inserted in the middle comes out clean.
When desired, top with the sugar and whipped cream from the confectioners.

## Cherry crumble

Ingredients
3 Cups (450 g) of bruised and halved cherries
2 cups of maple syrup
1 tbsp unmelted butter
1/2 tsp optional almond extract
4 Tbsp pinched granola

DIRECTIONS

The Air Fryer is preheated to 350F/180C

Mix the cherries, maple syrup, non-dairy oil, and almond extract (if used) together and apply a healthy baking pan or dish to Air Fryer.

Place the cherry crisp in the air fryer and cook until the cherries are fried to your taste for 15 minutes. While cooking, stir the cherry mixture at least once.

Open the Air Fryer basket when done, and add the granola on top of the cooked cherries.

Cook another 2-3 mins.

Serve warm and with some non-dairy ice cream on the side, this Air Fryer Cherry Crisp.

www.ingramcontent.com/pod-product-compliance
Lightning Source LLC
Chambersburg PA
CBHW081119080526
44587CB00021B/3671